Progress™
English Language Arts

4

Sadlier School

Cover: *Series Design:* Studio Montage; *Title design:* Quarasan, Inc. **Photo Credits:** *Cover:* Getty Images/Don Tremain: *bottom left.* iStockphoto.com/888photography: *right.* Used under license from Shutterstock.com/CrackerClips Stock Media: *center;* nikolarisim: *background;* rzymuR: *top left. Interior:* age fotostock/Blend Images/Dave and Les Jacobs: 40 *top;* Blend Images/Jose Luis Pelaez Inc: 148 *top,* 216 *top;* Corbis/Randy Faris: 53, 55; Huntstock: 98 *top;* Michael S. Nolan: 8 *top right;* Tetra Images/Jamie Grill; VStock LLC: 192 *top.* Alamy/Blend Images/JGI/Jamie Grill: 84 *top;* Paul S. Bartholemew: 127, 129; Nancy Hoyt Belcher: 246; Cultura Creative: 230 *top;* Phil Degginger: 75; Image Source/Sverre Haugland: 182; ImageState/Pictor International: 252; jvphoto: 8 *bottom right;* Richard Levine: 158; Photos 12: 130; Craig Ruttle: 156–157; Kevin Schafer: 64; Stock Montage, Inc.: 162 *top;* Stocktrek Images, Inc./John Parrot: 54 *top;* Tetra Images: 54 *top.* Corbis: 8 *bottom left,* 171 *top;* Bettmann: 169, 170; Bob Jacobson: 166; Dusko Despotovic: 180. Dreamstime.com/Beata Becla: 245; Ihar Balaikin: 169 *inset;* Cvandyke: 168, 169 *background;* Mikhail Kusayev: 83, 85; Lavenderphoto: 245; Paul Lemke: 56, 150; Tanja Rosso: 251. Fotolia.com/il-fede: 244; kmiragaya: 178 *top;* Cecila Lim: 257.Getty Images/AFP/YOSHIKAZU TSUNO: 242; Photo Researchers, Inc.: 154; Photodisc: 130 *inset;* SuperStock: 132; Richard Wahlstrom: 239. The Image Works/Fujiphotos: 177, 179. iStockphoto.com/gregobagel: 278. NASA: 229, 231; ESA/Hubble Heritage Team (STScI/AURA): 233; JPL-Caltech: 215, 220; JPL-Caltech/MSSS: 220. National Park Service Digital Image Archives: 76. REUTERS/Mainichi Shimbun: 72. Science Source/Friedrich Sauer: 8 *top left.* Used under license from Shutterstock.com/Antonio Abrignani: 131; a-poselenov: 171 *bottom;* Stephane Bidouze: 60; Lim ChewHow: 265, 275, 277; Iakov Filimonov: 18 *inset;* Jana Guothova: 10 *bottom,* 40 *bottom,* 54 *bottom,* 84 *bottom,* 98 *bottom,* 128 *bottom,* 148 *bottom,* 178 *bottom,* 192 *bottom,* 216 *bottom,* 230 *bottom;* Martin M303: 57; mikenorton: 58; Monkey Business Images: 128 *top;* nikolarisim: 1; Mahesh Patil: 265 *inset,* 275 *inset;* photobar: 250; R-studio: 162 *bottom,* 163. Smithsonian Institution/Division of Work and Industry, National Museum of American History: 18. SuperStock/Image Source: 147, 149. Courtesy of the U.S. Geological Survey, Austin Post: 74; photo by Karen M.L. Morgan: 88. Wikimedia Commons/Jim Henderson: 160. **Text Credit:** Common Core State Standards Copyright © 2010. National Governors Association Center for Best Practices and Council of Chief State School Officers. All rights reserved. **Illustration Credits:** Samantha Asri: 30, 31, 32. Tom Bonson: 200, 201, 202. Janet Broxon: 204. Peter Bull Art Studio: 19, 20, 22, 100, 101, 102, 104, 106, 107, 108, 110, 112, 113, 114, 116, 118, 119, 120, 232, 233, 248. Diane Greenseid: 11, 206, 207, 208. George Hamblin: 62, 63, 66, 68, 69, 70. Ted Hammond: 41, 42, 44. Red Hansen: 12, 13, 14, 16. Joe LeMonnier: 86, 151, 234, 236, 238, 241. Jamie Pogue: 24, 25, 26, 28. Q2A Media: 193, 195, 196, 198. Jason Wolff: 99. Eric Young: 163, 164.

For additional online resources, go to sadlierconnect.com.

William H. Sadlier, Inc.
9 Pine Street
New York, NY 10005-4700

Printed in the United States of America.
ISBN: 978-1-4217-3054-7
1 2 3 4 5 6 7 8 9 WEBC 18 17 16 15 14

CONTENTS

Welcome 8

Unit 1

Reading Literature:
Key Ideas and Details

Progress Check/Home Connect 9

Essential Question 11

Key Ideas and Details

Drawing Inferences 12

Determining Theme and Summarizing 18

Describing Characters, Settings, and Events 24

Close Reading: *Moving to a New World* 30

Connect Across Texts 35

Language

Using Context Clues 36

Unit 1 Review 37

Performance Task . . . . ONLINE

Unit 2

Text Types and Purposes:
Write Fictional Narratives

Progress Check/Home Connect 39

Essential Question 41

Write Fictional Narratives 42

Establishing a Situation • Introducing a Narrator or Characters • Using Dialogue and Descriptions of Actions • Using Transitional Words and Phrases • Providing a Conclusion

Language

Complete Sentences 46

Fragments 47

Run-on Sentences 48

Commas and Quotation Marks in Dialogue 49

Speaking and Listening 50

Unit 2 Review 51

Unit 3 | **Reading Informational Text:**
Key Ideas and Details

Progress Check/Home Connect 53
Essential Question 55

Key Ideas and Details
   Drawing Inferences 56
   Determining the Main Idea and Summarizing 62
   Explaining Events and Ideas 68
   Close Reading: *Volcanoes: Nature's Fire* 74
   Connect Across Texts 79

Language
   Affixes 80

Unit 3 Review 81
Performance Task . . . . (ONLINE)

Unit 4 | **Text Types and Purposes:**
Write Informative/Explanatory Texts

Progress Check/Home Connect 83
Essential Question 85
Write Informative/Explanatory Texts 86
   *Introducing a Topic • Grouping Related Information
   • Developing the Topic • Using Linking Words and
   Phrases • Using Precise Language • Providing a
   Concluding Statement*

Language
   Prepositional Phrases 90
   Progressive Forms of Verbs 91
   Precise Words and Phrases 92
   Order of Adjectives 93

Speaking and Listening 94

Unit 4 Review 95

Unit 5 | **Reading Literature:**
Craft and Structure

Progress Check/Home Connect 97
Essential Question 99

continued next page

Craft and Structure

Determining Word Meanings 100

Explaining Structural Elements 106

Comparing and Contrasting Points of View 112

Close Reading: *James Armistead: Spying for
the Revolution* 118

Connect Across Texts 123

Language

Figurative Language 124

Unit 5 Review 125

Performance Task . . . . (ONLINE)

Unit 6 Research to Build and Present Knowledge: Write Evidence-Based Essays

Progress Check/Home Connect 127

Essential Question 129

Writing Evidence-Based Essays 130
*Introducing a Topic • Describing in Depth a Character, Setting,
or Event • Drawing on Evidence to Support Analysis • Using
Quotations as Evidence • Providing a Concluding Statement*

Language

Commas and Quotation Marks in Direct Quotations 134

Relative Pronouns 135

Relative Adverbs 136

Punctuation for Effect 137

Speaking and Listening 138

Unit 6 Review 139

Unit 7 Reading Informational Text: Craft and Structure

Progress Check/Home Connect 147

Essential Question 149

Craft and Structure

Determining Word Meanings 150

Describing Text Structures 156

Comparing and Contrasting Events and Topics 162

Close Reading: *Helping the Union* 168

Connect Across Texts 173

continued next page

Language

   Synonyms and Antonyms 174

Unit 7 Review 175

Performance Task . . . . (ONLINE)

Unit 8	Text Types and Purposes: Write Opinion Pieces

Progress Check/Home Connect 177

Essential Question 179

Write Opinion Pieces 180

    Introducing the Topic • Stating an Opinion • Providing Reasons
    That Support the Opinion • Using Linking Words and Phrases
    • Providing a Concluding Statement

Language

   Formal and Informal English 184

   Frequently Confused Words 185

   Modal Auxiliaries 186

Speaking and Listening 188

Unit 8 Review 189

Unit 9	Reading Literature: Integration of Knowledge and Ideas

Progress Check/Home Connect 191

Essential Question 193

Integration of Knowledge and Ideas

   Making Connections Between Texts 194

   Comparing and Contrasting Themes and Topics 200

   Close Reading: *Pecos Bill and Slue-Foot Sue* 206

   Connect Across Texts 211

Language

   Idioms, Adages, and Proverbs 212

Unit 9 Review 213

Performance Task . . . . (ONLINE)

Unit 10	Research to Build and Present Knowledge: Write Research Reports

Progress Check/Home Connect 215

Essential Question 217

continued next page

Write Research Reports 218

Conducting Short Research Reports About a Topic • Gathering Relevant Information from Sources • Introducing a Topic • Grouping Related Information • Developing the Topic • Providing a Concluding Statement

Language

Commas in Compound Sentences 223

Capitalization 224

Spelling 225

Speaking and Listening 226

Unit 10 Review 227

Unit 11 Reading Informational Text:
Integration of Knowledge and Ideas

Progress Check/Home Connect 229

Essential Question 231

Integration of Knowledge and Ideas

Interpreting Visual Information 232

Analyzing Reasons and Evidence 238

Integrating Information from Texts 244

Close Reading: *The Robot Cheetah* 250

Connect Across Texts 255

Language

Roots 256

Unit 11 Review 257

Performance Task . . . . ONLINE

Performance Task 1 141

Performance Task 2 259

Foundational Skills Handbook 265

Writing Handbook 275

Glossary 284

Index 288

Welcome

You have an exciting year ahead of you. You will be reading all kinds of different passages—in all sorts of formats—about interesting topics, such as quests, scientific discoveries, and making the world a better place. You'll learn how to read more carefully so you can better understand what you read.

Writing is important, too. Suppose you want to describe a character from a story you read, or compare two versions of the same legend. If you write well, you can communicate these ideas clearly. You will also see other students' writing and try to improve on it or use it as a model for your own work.

This book, *Progress English Language Arts*, will help you improve in both reading and writing, and maybe even do better in school. That's why it's called *progress*.

Have a great year!

Introducing UNIT 1

Have you ever taken a journey? A journey can mean adventure. It can mean danger. It can even mean laughs! In this unit about difficult journeys, you will learn how authors make stories interesting.

In the upcoming stories, the authors use details to create interesting events and characters. In some stories, you will look for ways that details help you make inferences about the story. In another selection, you will use details to help you figure out the theme, or message, that the author wants to share. You also will look for details that help you connect with characters and events in a story.

Understanding these basic elements of literature will help you enjoy these stories. It also will help you appreciate the difficult journeys that these characters take. Let the journeys begin!

Progress Check Can I?

Before Unit 1

After Unit 1

☐ ☐ Use details to make inferences about what a story says.

☐ ☐ Determine the theme of a story.

☐ ☐ Summarize events in a story.

☐ ☐ Describe the characters, settings, and events in a story.

☐ ☐ Use context clues to determine the meaning of a word.

HOME ◆ CONNECT...

When reading literature, effective readers pay attention both to what the author says and to what the author implies. As you read a story with your child, pause to encourage your child to state some conclusions and **inferences** about the story's characters and events, based on details in the text. Compare his or her thoughts with your own.

The **theme** of a story is the message or "lesson" that the author wants to convey. Considering the conflict that a story presents and how it is resolved can help readers determine the story's theme. As you read a story together, ask your child to **summarize** key story events. At the end, discuss the message that the author seems to convey.

In order to be engaged readers, students need to think about the **characters, settings, and events** in a story. As you read together, ask your child active questions about details in the story—for example: What does the main character look like? When and where does this story take place? What just happened on this page?

On the Go: Invite your child to go on an adventure by looking for stories in the world around you. Start with a recent family event: Ask your child to name the setting and characters and to summarize the plot as if the event were a story that he or she had read. As you travel together in the community, challenge your child to suggest stories that might take place in settings that you pass.

IN THIS UNIT, YOUR CHILD WILL...

- Learn how to identify the details that make a story clear.
- Use details to make inferences about a story.
- Learn how to determine the theme of a text.
- Summarize a text.
- Use details from a story to describe the characters, setting, and events.
- Use context, or nearby words and sentences, as clues to determine the meaning of unfamiliar words and phrases.
- Compare and contrast four texts on the same theme: an adventure story, an example of historical fiction, a science fiction story, and a realistic fiction story.

WAYS TO HELP YOUR CHILD

Show your child how to identify the important details in a story. Whether you are reading together, watching a movie or TV show, or discussing the day's events, help your child increase his or her understanding by actively questioning and summarizing what he or she sees and hears.

ONLINE

For more Home Connect activities, continue online at sadlierconnect.com

Reading Literature: Key Ideas and Details

Essential Question:
How do authors use details to make a story more interesting?

Drawing Inferences 12

Determining Theme and Summarizing 18

Describing Characters, Settings,
and Events 24

Close Reading 30

Connect Across Texts 35

Language: Context Clues 36

Unit 1 Review 37

DRAWING INFERENCES

WORDS TO KNOW

landscape

opportunity

An **inference** is an educated guess, or conclusion, based on evidence from the text.

CITE EVIDENCE

A **Details** in a story are pieces of information that help you understand the characters, settings, and events. Find and underline the details in paragraph 5 that help you understand Paul.

B You can use details to make **inferences** about a story. Review the details about Paul. Then circle the detail in paragraph 8 that tells Jackson's reaction to Paul. What inference can you make about these two scouts?

Into the Grand Canyon

(Genre: Adventure Story)

1   "Jackson, let's go!"

2   "Sorry, Mr. Anderson; I was just gathering my supplies."

3   "Way to be prepared, Jackson!" Mr. Anderson, our troop leader, arranged this hike for us, and he made us do some intense training before we could go. A back-country hike in the Grand Canyon is an incredible **opportunity**, but it can also be a little dangerous. Mr. Anderson is giving us instructions as I join the rest of the troop.

4   "We are two miles from our campsite, and the other troop should already be there. Let's stay aware of the **landscape**, and let's stay together."

5   While we are getting ready, I look for my best friend, Paul. Paul is a genius. He can beat any video game, fix any computer problem, and set up any smartphone. He doesn't really do much outdoors, though.

6   Paul is studying his cell phone. "What are you doing?" I ask. "Do you have service down here?"

7   "Enough to play my video games."

8   I frown with annoyance. "Paul, we are getting ready to hike through the Grand Canyon, so how can you even think about video games?" I snatch his cell phone and hold it high over my head.

Guided Instruction

9   "Hey! What was that for?"

10   "We are about to have an adventure, and you don't want to miss it. I'll give this back to you when we reach camp!"

11   I wait for Paul to argue with me, but he starts laughing. "All right, you win. Anyway, I can't imagine what my mom will say if I tell her that all I remember about the Grand Canyon is my high score!"

12   Each member of our troop has a special responsibility. I'm in charge of the compass, while Paul is responsible for following the maps to make sure we are on the right trail. Paul checks the map and reminds us of our course. "In order to reach our campsite, we need to head due west."

13   I grab my compass, locate due west, and point off in the distance. "That trail over there is ours."

14   But before we can begin, someone yells from behind us, "Hey, hang on!"

15   A park ranger jogs over to Mr. Anderson and asks, "Are these scouts hiking that trail?"

16   "We sure are."

CITE EVIDENCE

C Authors use details to help bring a story to life for the reader. Reread paragraph 12. Then underline the details about the scouts' responsibilities.

D Making inferences about a text is different from understanding what a text tells you directly. Box a sentence on this page that gives details about Paul's mother. What does the sentence say about her directly? What can you infer from that?

Comprehension Check

Why has the park ranger stopped the troop? Look for details in paragraphs 14–16 that can help you explain your inference.

be cose las wech thay had aproblem sowe he chete

DRAWING INFERENCES

Guided Practice

WORDS TO KNOW

flash flood

species

sprained

terrain

CITE EVIDENCE

A Circle the details in paragraphs 18–21 that name the kinds of animals the scouts see in the Grand Canyon.

B In paragraphs 23–26, underline the details that tell how Jackson feels. What inference can you make about Jackson's injuries?

Into the Grand Canyon *continued*

17 "I wanted to warn you that we had a **flash flood** here last week, and it washed out some **terrain**. The footing on the trail may be difficult."

18 We finally set out on the trail, and we are having a great time. Even Paul gets into the spirit, shouting every time he spots a lizard or squirrel. He even sees some rare **species**—a baby mule deer and its mom, and some coyote tracks on the trail.

19 We have been hiking for about an hour when Paul suddenly yells, "Hey, look up there!"

20 We look where Paul is pointing, and we see a giant bird perched on a rock wall above us.

21 "I don't believe it!" Mr. Anderson exclaims. "That's a California condor, one of the rarest birds in the world!"

22 Everyone starts snapping pictures. I can't believe our luck, and I'm trying to get as many pictures as I can, too. That is probably why I don't notice that the trail in front of me has washed out.

23 One minute I'm walking toward the condor's perch; the next minute, I'm at the bottom of a ditch. I can't catch my breath, and my left ankle hurts.

24 I hear Paul yell, "Jackson!" and he and Mr. Anderson slide down beside me.

25 "Are you hurt, Jackson?"

26 "My ankle is starting to throb. I'm sorry, Mr. Anderson. I was so busy looking at the condor that I forgot to watch the trail."

27   "Don't worry about that, Jackson. Let's get you on your feet."

28   I try to stand up, but the weight on my ankle is too much. "It's no good, Mr. Anderson; I think it's **sprained**."

29   "I guess we are going to find out how much you learned during our training." He calls to the other troop members. "Gentlemen, we have our first challenge, as it appears that Jackson has sprained his ankle. What are the next steps?"

Comprehension Check

1. In paragraph 17, what can the hikers infer from the park ranger's warning that the footing on the trail may be difficult?

   a. The scouts will have to walk with extra caution.

   b. The scouts should stay off of the trail.

   c. The scouts do not have the right shoes for hiking.

   d. The scouts should not hike in the Grand Canyon.

2. In paragraph 29, why does Mr. Anderson say, "I guess we are going to find out how much you learned during our training"?

   a. He is not sure what to do about a sprained ankle.

   b. He wants the scouts to work together in an emergency.

   c. He doubts that the other scouts can help Jackson.

   d. He is upset that Jackson's carelessness has made everyone stop.

3. Work with a partner. Based on the details you have read so far, make an inference about the training the scouts had before leaving on this hike. Explain your answer.

When thag whent thay wer lots in the thasard

DRAWING INFERENCES

Into the Grand Canyon *continued*

WORDS TO KNOW

assemble

immobile

thermal

CITE EVIDENCE

A Underline the details in paragraph 37 that identify the actions Paul takes when Jackson is injured.

B Why does Paul ask if Jackson has really sprained his ankle? Circle dialogue on page 17 that helps you make an inference about this issue.

30   There's a short pause, and then everyone starts yelling out answers.

31   "Make sure Jackson is warm. We don't want him to go into shock."

32   "Splint the ankle to keep it **immobile**."

33   "Give him plenty of water!"

34   Before I can even react, everyone gets to work. Someone throws a **thermal** blanket over my shoulders while someone else hands me a water bottle. Our first aid team looks at my ankle, elevating my foot and maneuvering the splint over my pants.

35   I notice that Paul is rifling around in my backpack. "Hey," I say, "why are you going through my stuff while I'm lying here, helpless?"

36   Paul grins. "You have the compass and my cell phone, buddy. Now let me do my job—getting you safely to our campsite."

37   To everyone's surprise, Paul turns out to be great in an emergency. He double-checks the maps and the compass. He also **assembles** some of the other scouts to clean the debris from the trail ahead of us. He even manages to find a spot with cell phone service so Mr. Anderson can call the leader of our partner troop and let him know what happened.

38   Before long, we are back on the trail. It takes two scouts to hold me up, but we manage. Slowly, we make our way to our campsite.

39   That night, as we all gather around the campfire, I thank Paul for his help.

40   He looks at me out of the corner of his eye and says, "Hey, man, I have to ask you a question. You really did sprain your ankle, right?"

41   "Of course I did! Why in the world would you ask that?"

42   "Well, you did promise me an adventure, and I think that was pretty exciting!"

43   I laugh loudly. "You got that right! Still missing your video games, Paul?"

44   "No way! Even video games don't have *this* kind of action!"

Comprehension Check   (MORE ONLINE) **sadlierconnect.com**

1. What can you infer about Paul based on how he responds to Jackson's injury?

   a. He is worried about which trail direction to take.

   b. He is not sure what to do in an emergency.

   c. He would rather be playing video games.

   d. He is a good friend and a good leader.

2. What can you infer from story details about the purpose of a thermal blanket (paragraph 34)?

   a. It is meant to help a person cool off.

   b. It is meant to increase a person's body warmth.

   c. It is meant to keep an injured person calm.

   d. It is meant to keep the sun off of a person's skin.

3. In paragraph 40, Paul asks whether Jackson really sprained his ankle. Based on your reading, make an inference about what Paul is really trying to say.

   _____

   _____

   _____

   _____

Guided Instruction

WORDS TO KNOW

gale

hull

merchant ship

> The **theme** of a story is the message or "lesson" that an author wants to convey to the reader.

CITE EVIDENCE

A Most stories present a **theme**, or message. Underline details in paragraph 1 that may help you determine the theme of this story.

B When you **summarize** a story, you give a short description of what you just read. Circle the name of the person who is telling this story. Then summarize what she says on the first page of this story.

On Board the *Isaac Webb*

(Genre: Historical Fiction)

1   I am lying in my small bunk in our cabin, my stomach churning every time a wave crashes against the ship's **hull**. We have been sailing for almost two months, and it has been weeks since we felt smooth seas. We hit a **gale** in October, and the weather never seemed to improve after that. Luckily, we should arrive in New York any day now. The ship starts to sway again, and I bury my head in my pillow. Suddenly, I hear the ship's warning bell sound! My father rushes into my room. He yells, "Lisbeth, put on your life jacket! We've run aground!"

2   We departed from Liverpool, England, on September 22, 1868. I was very excited to be sailing for New York. The *Isaac Webb* was the largest ship I had ever seen. I couldn't believe we were going to be sailing on it for a month. My brothers are both older than I am, and they were trying hard to act bored. Still, I could tell they were as excited as the rest of us. This was the first time my brothers and I had ever traveled on a **merchant ship**.

3   My father has been on merchant ships many times. He works for the Black Ball Line, the company that owns the *Isaac Webb*. He often travels back and forth between England and America. This time, however, would be different. We were all going with him: me, my mother, my brothers, and even our nanny, Amelia. That's because this wasn't a business trip. We were all moving to New York!

4   According to my father, the crossing from England is always rough. For the first few days, all I did was wander the decks with Nanny Amelia. We watched the stormy sea and sky, and I made drawings in my sketchbook. Although I wanted to talk to the merchant sailors, Nanny Amelia said that we must not disturb them. She explained that they had more important things to do than chat with a 10-year-old girl. I noticed, though, that her warning to me didn't keep her from smiling at every sailor on deck!

CITE EVIDENCE

C Circle the sentence in paragraph 3 that you think best summarizes the whole paragraph. How can you tell which details are most important?

D Continue thinking about a possible theme for this story. Underline details in paragraph 4 that add to what you noted on page 18. Think about how this information might help you determine the theme.

Comprehension Check

Review paragraphs 1–4. Then, in your own words, summarize the story events that happen in these first four paragraphs.

Guided Practice

WORDS TO KNOW

ominous

provisions

route

CITE EVIDENCE

A In paragraphs 5–8, the author introduces a problem that helps to develop the theme. Underline details that help make the problem clear.

B Circle the date in paragraph 8. Then summarize paragraphs 5–8 with a partner. Take out the small details and discuss only the main events.

5   By the end of the second week, my brothers and I were bored. Most of the 350 passengers on the ship sleep down in steerage, which is belowdecks. There are only 10 passenger cabins like ours on the ship. We tried sneaking down to steerage. We wanted to see if there were any other boys and girls. However, we didn't even reach the door before Nanny Amelia caught us!

6   On the 10th of October, everything changed. That's the day we ran into the worst storm to hit the merchant ship **route** this season. When we woke up in the morning, the skies had become black and **ominous**. The ship's steward told us to stay in our cabins and to make sure our life jackets were always with us. And then the storm hit! I can't describe the force from the waves crashing over the decks. The sound of the wind screaming through the air made my eardrums feel as if they were going to burst!

7   After about a week, the worst of the weather died down. The ship had been damaged by the winds. The crew was forced to slow down and try to make repairs. Father helped the crew however he could.

8   By November 12, we had completely run out of food. Father said the passengers in steerage were getting restless. He worried about the crew's ability to get us to New York in time.

9   Just when things seemed at their lowest, we had some luck. The Canadian ship *Brazil* was passing by and saw that we were in distress. Its crew restocked our **provisions**. Now we had enough supplies to make it to New York.

10   And that brings us to today, November 17. We are off the coast of New Jersey, heading for New York. We are moving slowly, still fighting the seas, when I hear the alarm.

Comprehension Check

1. Which fact from the story, so far, helps make the theme clear?

   a. Nanny Amelia keeps a strict watch on the children.

   b. Lisbeth is excited to be moving to New York.

   c. The passengers face a storm and a food shortage.

   d. The *Brazil* gives provisions to the *Isaac Webb*.

2. If you were summarizing the story so far, which of these details would you NOT include?

   a. Lisbeth's father has made many ocean voyages.

   b. The seas are rough at first, and then a storm strikes.

   c. The *Isaac Webb* is damaged and needs repairs.

   d. The passengers are upset when the food runs out.

3. With a partner, discuss what you think is the theme of the story. Use details from the text to support your answer.

In the text I think the theme should be Lisbeth was so excited to go to newyork.

DETERMINING THEME AND SUMMARIZING

On Board the *Isaac Webb* *continued*

WORDS TO KNOW

anticipation

destination

sandbank

CITE EVIDENCE

A Circle the paragraph on page 22 that describes the solution to the main problem.

B At the end of paragraph 17, you are ready to summarize the entire story. Underline some of the main events in paragraphs 11–16. Which earlier events are still important enough to include in the summary?

11   Father bursts into our cabin and shouts, "We've run aground!" He orders us to put on our life jackets, and he takes my brothers to the deck to help. Mother, Nanny Amelia, and I sit down to wait for them to return.

12   My father and brothers finally come down for the night, just as I am going crazy waiting for news. Father explains that the ship is stuck on a **sandbank**, too far off the coast to dock. The captain has called for help. Father tells us to prepare for a long wait while other ships come and try to tow us out.

13   I wake up the next morning, eager to be on our way. I am tired and ready to get off this ship. Mother and Nanny Amelia try to keep me entertained, and I do my best to be cheerful. We all try to be brave.

14   The morning of November 19 is the first sunny day in a month. Before I am even out of bed, my brothers wake me up.

15   "Get up, Lisbeth. Father says the rescue ships are on their way. We get to watch!"

16   I rush to get on my clothing and life jacket. Then we all head to the main deck, where two ships have arrived to help us out. I watch, excitedly, as the *Isaac Webb is* attached to the *Philip* and the *Rescue*. I hold my breath with **anticipation** as the two ships begin towing the *Isaac Webb* off of the sandbank. And I cheer excitedly when we are at sea again. We are headed for New York!

17   Father promises that we will be towed into the harbor by day's end. He says we will dock at the Black Ball Line's port on the East River. My excitement builds. Even though this has been a difficult journey, we are almost at our **destination**. One adventure is behind us, but the next is just about to begin!

Comprehension Check

(MORE ONLINE) **sadlierconnect.com**

1. Which words might you use to describe Lisbeth in a summary of paragraphs 11–12?

   a. brave but lonely

   b. bored and curious

   c. patient and brave

   d. restless and afraid

2. Which of these possible titles best expresses the theme of this story?

   a. "Finding a Friend"

   b. "Staying Strong"

   c. "The Mysteries of Nature"

   d. "Past, Present, and Future"

3. In your own words, write a short summary of the story. Include only the most important details and events.

_____

_____

_____

_____

_____

Guided Instruction

WORDS TO KNOW

intensely

lecture

orbiting

You can use details to describe the **characters**, **settings**, and **events** in a story.

CITE EVIDENCE

A A **character** is a person in a short story, novel, or play. Find and underline the names of the characters in paragraphs 1–3.

B The **setting** of a story is the place and time in which the story happens. In paragraph 1, circle a "time" detail. What "place" details can you find on this page?

Straight Up, and Straight Back Down

(Genre: Science Fiction)

1   In the year 2040, David Rivera, astronaut and father, decided to be the first person to go to outer space with his entire family. David knew some very important people, who thought his idea was great, and they built him a spaceship. Of course, David forgot about one thing. He forgot to ask his ten-year-old daughter if she wanted to go into outer space, which she definitely did not! That daughter is me, Sara Rivera, and David Rivera is my dad.

2   You might believe that going to outer space would be the best thing that ever happened to me, but you would be wrong. Just think, for a minute, about what it is like to go to space. You have to leave all of your friends behind, and you have to eat nasty space food—no delicious hamburgers up there. You have to spend months in a tiny capsule with your parents! And don't even ask about going to the bathroom. Trust me, you do not want to know.

3   So, here I am, **orbiting** miles above Earth, listening to my mother **lecture** me, again, on how I am wasting this great opportunity.

4   "Sara Mariana Rivera, your father went to great lengths to make this adventure happen for all of us, and think about the amazing stories you will have when we get back home! Lots of kids would be thrilled to get a chance like this."

5   "Well, I'm not lots of kids, and it's not as if we are going anywhere special! It's just straight up into space and then straight back down."

6   Just as I am about to launch into a super-sized meltdown, complete with tears, the ship jerks **intensely**, and the room starts spinning—slowly, at first, and then faster.

7   "What's going on, Mom?"

8   "Just hold on, Sara! Hold on tight!"

9   Before I can answer her, I see lights dancing in front of my eyes. I feel lightheaded, and then everything goes black.

10 When I wake up, I can feel a hand stroking my forehead. "Mom, I had the worst dream," I whisper. "We were on a spaceship, and I passed out."

Comprehension Check

Think about the details in paragraphs 1–10. How would you describe Sara's mother so far?

CITE EVIDENCE

C A story also contains **events**, or actions that occur as the story unfolds. Reread paragraph 6. Then circle one event that occurs in that paragraph.

D An author helps readers learn more about the characters in a story through words, thoughts, and actions. Underline Sara's complaining words on this page. What do those words help readers learn about Sara?

Guided Practice

Straight Up, and Straight Back Down *continued*

WORDS TO KNOW

focus

language

CITE EVIDENCE

A Find a detail in paragraph 11 that describes the new setting. Put a box around it.

B Circle details in paragraphs 11 and 15 that describe the character whom Sara calls "the green lady." Discuss those details.

11   Suddenly, everything comes into **focus**. I am in a large white room, and I see my mom in her red dress, with her yellow eyes and green skin, looking down at me. Wait a second: My mom doesn't have yellow eyes or green skin! The creature in front of me opens its mouth and says something like, "Heebie-jeebie, flib-goblin."

12   I shake my head and say, "I can't understand you."

13   Before the green lady can answer, I hear a voice from across the room, asking, "Sara, is that you?"

14   "Mom, where are you?"

15   The green lady picks me up with one hand, and that's when I realize she's about ten feet tall! She carries me easily, and sets me down between my parents.

16   "Mom and Dad, what happened?"

17   "We landed," my dad says, "but I'm not sure where."

18   In the meantime, the green lady has been observing us. "Blim-blam, zoobie?" she asks.

19   Puzzled, I turn to my dad. "What's she saying?"

20   "We haven't figured it out, Sara, but I think she's friendly."

21   The green creature opens her mouth again, but this time, instead of speaking, she starts to sing. It's the most beautiful music I have ever heard, and it makes me want to sing along.

22   Without thinking, I start to sing, even though I don't know the **language.** When I glance at my parents, I realize that we are all doing the same thing.

Comprehension Check

1. What do the nonsense words in paragraph 11 tell readers about the character called "the green lady"?

(a.) The green lady speaks a language that is unknown to Sara.

b. The green lady is just a baby, so she has not yet learned to talk.

c. The green lady cannot speak Sara's language clearly.

d. The green lady enjoys playing jokes on her visitors.

2. Based on what you read in the text, what event has most likely happened by the time paragraph 11 begins?

a. Sara has fallen asleep and is having a dream.

b. Sara's home has been invaded by aliens.

c. Sara's parents are playing a practical joke on her.

(d.) Sara was on board the spaceship when it crashed.

3. Work with a partner to write about the four characters in the story. Cite evidence to describe what you know about each of them.

My evidence is that Sara Sara was the little kid and she wasn't like other kids. David was sara father and David went out of space. The mom always go in Sara room and talk to sara about outer space.

Independent Practice

Straight Up, and Straight Back Down *continued*

WORDS TO KNOW

coordinate

universe

CITE EVIDENCE

A What events happen between the time Sara passes out and the time she wakes up in the green lady's room? Underline evidence in paragraph 27.

B Reread paragraphs 34–36. To what event does Sara's mother refer? What do her final words tell you about her as a character?

23   When the music stops, the green lady turns to us and asks, "Can you understand me now?"

24   "Whoa!" I exclaim. "What happened?"

25   "Music is the language of the **universe**. If we can understand each other in song, we can understand each other in everything."

26   My dad nods. "Can you tell us where we are, and what happened to our ship?"

27   "Your ship is fine. You were caught in a space storm, and it blew you to our planet. Now, I will return you to your ship."

28   "Wait!" my dad yells. "There is so much we can learn from each other. Can't we stay?"

29   "I'm sorry, but that's impossible. The storm that brought you here is almost over. You must return to your ship now, or you may never get home."

30   The green lady picks all of us up and carries us out of the room. She walks across what looks like a desert, past other green alien-things, to our ship.

31   The green lady sets us down and pats me on the back. "Go home to your planet and tell others what you have seen. Perhaps we will meet again someday."

32   "Thank you," my dad says.

33   We board our spaceship and settle into our seats. We sit, silently, in shock and amazement. My dad enters the **coordinates** for Earth into our navigation system, and we rise into the sky.

34   Finally, I find the right words. "Mom," I say, "remember that argument we had before the ship crashed?"

35   "You mean the one where you said we were going nowhere special, just straight up and straight down?"

36   "Yeah, that one. Can we just pretend I never said that?"

37   My mom starts to giggle. "Heebie-jeebie, flib-goblin," she says.

38   As our ship heads for home, we all burst into laughter.

Comprehension Check   (MORE ONLINE) **sadlierconnect.com**

1. Which of the following describes the setting where the green lady lives?

   a. a lush rain forest on Jupiter

   b. an ocean on Neptune

   c. an evergreen forest on Mars

   d. a desert on an unknown planet

2. Think back to the beginning of the story. What time period best fits the setting of this story?

   a. the present day

   b. the far-off future

   c. sometime in your adult life

   d. sometime in the ancient past

3. How does the characters' conversation at the end of the story help you understand the story's title?

   _____

   _____

   _____

   _____

Moving to a New World

(Genre: Realistic Fiction)

1   My name is Tran Vien Thai, but my friends call me "Ty." The first thing you need to know about me is that I live a double life. I'm a Vietnamese immigrant in America, and I live between two worlds. At home, I'm Tran, a boy who lives with his family and follows the traditions we brought from Vietnam. At school, I'm Ty, an average fourth-grader and baseball player.

2   About a year ago, I was living with my family on the outskirts of Hanoi, the capital of Vietnam. My father worked in a factory, while my mother and grandmother took care of the home and my baby sister. I went to school, did chores, and studied.

3   My favorite part of each day began when my father arrived home from work. Every evening, my father and I played baseball. I used to watch my father practice, amazed at what a great player he was. He could pitch harder, hit longer, and run faster than anyone else I had ever seen.

4   And then, one day, our lives changed. Some minor league baseball players and coaches from America came to Hanoi to visit the youth baseball camps. One afternoon, my father decided to go see the players work out. He was sitting in the outfield stands, watching practice, when a ball landed at his feet. My father grabbed the ball and sailed it across the field, hitting home plate.

5 One of the coaches recruited my father. Within a few months, my entire family relocated to America. My father was signed as a pitcher for the Jackson Generals, one of the Seattle Mariners' minor league teams, and we moved to Tennessee.

6 I was so excited to start school in America, I could hardly sleep the night before. In Vietnam, I could easily walk to the small school in our village, but now, I would ride a bus to school for the first time. I woke up early and quickly got dressed.

7 My grandmother, whom I call Ba, was already up. She was making lunch for me. It looked like she was putting *pho*, my favorite noodle soup, into a container for me. It smelled delicious, but I had a feeling American kids didn't eat *pho* for lunch. I tried to sneak by, but my grandmother has hearing like a wolf.

8 "Come here, Tran, and get your lunch."

9 "Ba, I have to catch the bus."

10 "Do not argue with me. We may be in America, but we are still Vietnamese."

11 I grabbed the lunch bag from my grandmother, hoping she would let me leave the house without another lecture. This was not my lucky day.

12 "Tran, what are you wearing?"

13 I glanced down at my clothes. "Jeans and a t-shirt. It's what all of the American boys wear."

14 "You will not show that kind of disrespect for your teacher. Get back to your room right now and change into something nicer." I knew there was no point in arguing, so I went back to my room and changed into a button-up shirt and khaki pants.

15 By the time I finished changing clothes, I was running late. I had to sprint to the bus stop! I boarded the bus and looked fretfully for an open seat. Every eye was on me, the new guy in the strange clothing. Everyone else was wearing t-shirts and jeans.

16 Things didn't improve once I got to class. My teacher couldn't pronounce my name correctly. She tried four times before I stopped her and said, "Just call me Ty."

17 Lunchtime was even worse. I didn't have any friends to sit with, and my homemade *pho* looked strange next to the other kids' sandwiches. I ate my lunch as quickly as I could and then went back to the classroom to hide.

18 After that, I felt as if I didn't fit in anywhere. The kids seemed nice, but I didn't know what we had in common.

19 My father, however, was having a great time as a ballplayer. I couldn't wait to see him pitch his first game. When my dad took the pitcher's mound on Opening Day, I was more nervous than he was!

20 I forgot about the loneliness at school, missing my friends in Vietnam, and trying to learn about America. Instead, I just focused on the game. The batter came up to the box… my father pulled back… and he sailed one across the plate! Strike one!

21 I was cheering so loudly, I almost didn't hear my name being called: "Ty! Hey, Ty!"

22 My grandmother gave me a stern look. "Tran, I believe that young man is trying to get your attention, and he seems to think your name is Ty."

23 "That's my American name, Ba. But don't worry about it, because I don't really know him."

24 "Tran, you will not be rude to that young man. Go say hello."

25 I walked tentatively up the stands to where Marcus, a boy I recognized from class, was sitting with his family.

26 "Hey, Ty! I didn't know you liked baseball."

27 "I'm here to see my father pitch."

28 "What? Your father is the new hotshot pitcher? Why didn't you say so?"

29   "I didn't think anyone would care."

30   "Not care! Wow, do you have a lot to learn about America!"

31   I looked down and whispered, "I know." Then, I started to walk away. Marcus stopped me.

32   "Where are you going? I can't believe I have a friend whose dad is a baseball star! Wait until I tell the guys at school!"

33   It has been several months since Marcus became my friend. I have learned that I don't have to turn my back on my culture in order to find my new life in America. In fact, most of my American friends think my family is great. They're always asking me questions about life in Vietnam. I have learned a lot since we moved—not just about America, but about myself. Having a double life may not always be easy, but I wouldn't have it any other way.

Comprehension Check

1. Based on what you read in the story, which statement best describes the character of Tran's grandmother?

   a. She is very quiet and shy, and she rarely talks to Tran.

   b. She does not believe in tradition, and she wants to embrace all of American culture.

   c. She expects Tran to maintain his cultural traditions in his new home.

   d. She is angry that Tran's father moved the family to America.

2. Which statement best expresses the theme of this story?

   a. It is important to embrace both tradition and change.

   b. Leaving your home will make you an outcast forever.

   c. You should forget about your past and look only to the future.

   d. Baseball is the Great American Pastime.

3. The story does not describe Tran's father in detail. Still, you can make inferences about his relationship with Tran, based on details in the text. Describe Tran's relationship with his father. Support your ideas with details from the text.

_____

_____

_____

_____

_____

_____

_____

_____

4. Think about the most important details from the story. Summarize the story. Then, in a sentence, describe the story's theme, or message.

_____

_____

_____

_____

_____

_____

_____

_____

_____

Compare and Contrast Texts

In this unit, you read four texts that used details to tell stories about difficult journeys. Think about the kinds of journeys that characters in these stories experienced. Then choose two of the texts, and compare and contrast them using the T-chart below. List important details to show how the texts are similar or different. Be prepared to discuss your ideas with the class.

Similarities	Differences

Return to the Essential Question

How do authors use details to make a story more interesting?

In small groups or as a class, discuss the Essential Question. Think about what you have learned about character, setting, and events and about details, inferences, and themes. Use evidence from the four unit texts to answer the question.

Using Context Clues

Guided Instruction As you are reading a text, you will sometimes come across unfamiliar words or phrases. When this happens, look for **context clues**—clues in the same sentence or nearby sentences—that can help you figure out the meanings.

Read this sentence from "Moving to a New World": *It looked like she was putting* pho, *my favorite noodle soup, into a container for me.* You may never have heard of *pho*, but a clue is right next to it: *my favorite noodle soup. Pho* is a kind of noodle soup!

Sometimes the clue is more of an inference. Read these sentences from the same story: *By the time I finished changing clothes, I was running late. I had to sprint to the bus stop!* If you do not know the word *sprint*, think about this: To make sure that he doesn't miss the bus, Tran will probably hurry. *Sprint*, then, has to do with hurrying or moving quickly.

Guided Practice Use context clues to figure out the meaning of each word in **bold type**. The examples are from "Moving to a New World."

1. One afternoon, my father decided to go see the players **work out**.
   _____

2. My father grabbed the ball and **sailed** it across the field, hitting home plate. _____

3. Within a few months, my entire family **relocated** to America.
   _____

Independent Practice Use context clues to figure out the meanings of these other words from "Moving to a New World." Then choose two of the words and write a sentence for each of them. Try to include a context clue in each sentence.

    immigrant (paragraph 1)   **fretfully** (paragraph 15)

    recruited (paragraph 5)   **fit in** (paragraph 18)

_____

_____

Read the following adventure story. The story details help describe the characters and setting in the story. They also help you make inferences about the text. Then answer the questions on pages 37 and 38.

Race to the Treasure

(Genre: Adventure Story)

1   Becca ran as fast as she could, her long blond hair plastered to her face in the rain. She could hear her father's footsteps slightly ahead of her in the forest. She slid in the mud once and caught herself, but then she slid again. This time, she lost her footing completely and plummeted down a steep slope into a deep pit.

2   Her father screamed, "Are you hurt?"

3   Becca tried to answer, but she couldn't catch her breath. Lifting her head out of the mud, she saw the walls of a deep hole.

4   She wiped the mud from her eyes—and then gasped in shock.

5   All around her were riches beyond imagination. Precious jewels lay next to chests filled with gold, and silver bracelets rested on diamond-encrusted tiaras.

6   *We did it,* Becca thought. *What luck. We finally found the lost treasure!*

7   From above, her father yelled again: "Becca!"

8   Becca struggled to her feet and began to answer.

Fill in the circle of the correct answer choice.

1. What is one detail about Becca that appears in paragraph 1?

   ○ long blond hair

   ○ high-pitched laugh

   ○ fifteen years old

   ○ runs very slowly

2. The setting for this story is

   ○ a rocky seashore.

   ○ an oasis in the desert.

   ○ a forest and a pit.

   ○ a cabin in the woods.

3. Becca's thoughts show that she and her father were looking for

    ○ a lost family member.   ○ a lost tiara.

    ○ a lost treasure.   ○ a lost diamond.

4. What does the word *plastered* in paragraph 1 mean?

    ○ stuck with concrete   ○ crafted by an artist

    ○ made of plaster   ○ pressed hard against something

5. Underline the details that describe the setting in paragraph 5.

6. What does paragraph 8 tell readers about Becca's character?

_____

7. What inference can you make about how Becca and her father feel about each other? How can you tell?

_____

_____

8. Use context clues to suggest a word or phrase that could replace the word *plummeted* in paragraph 1.

_____

9. From details in the story, what do you think will happen next? Which details help you make that inference?

_____

_____

_____

10. What theme do you find in this story? Use text evidence to explain.

_____

_____

_____

Introducing UNIT 2

Just about everyone likes to listen to stories. Stories can be fun to write and share. In this unit about difficult journeys, you will learn how to write an effective fictional narrative, or short story.

To write a fictional narrative, make up a sequence of events that readers will enjoy. The events can be things that happen in real life, or they can be very imaginative. Think of interesting characters, too. Then show the events in a way that makes sense. Use dialogue and details to help readers understand the characters' experiences and feelings. Finally, be sure to provide a conclusion that wraps up the story events.

An effective fictional narrative should have a clear sequence of events, connected by transitional words. Use descriptive details and sensory language to make the characters' experiences come to life. The writing also should be grammatically correct.

Progress Check *Can I?*

Before Unit 2 ↓ / After Unit 2 ↓

	Before	After
Write a fictional narrative about real or imagined events.	☐	☐
Establish a story situation and characters.	☐	☐
Organize story events in a natural way, and include a conclusion.	☐	☐
Use transitional words to connect events.	☐	☐
Use dialogue and include descriptive details.	☐	☐
Identify and correct sentence fragments and run-on sentences.	☐	☐
Correctly use commas and quotation marks in dialogue.	☐	☐

HOME✦CONNECT...

In this unit, children will learn about writing a story that they have made up—that is, to write effective **narrative fiction**. The stories can be set in any place or time, and they encourage young writers to exercise their imagination. Invite your child to share the story that he or she writes for this unit and other original stories that may follow.

Realistic fiction includes events that actually could happen. Historical fiction weaves real people, places, and events into an entertaining tale. Science fiction often imagines future technology and worlds yet to be discovered. Talk about the kinds of stories that your child enjoys most.

As your child reads different fictional narratives, ask about each story's **setting**, **narrator**, and **characters**. Discuss how **dialogue** and **descriptive details** make a story enjoyable. Ask your child what he or she might put into the story if he or she were writing it.

Apply the discussion to other kinds of storytelling. For example, ask what dialogue your child might write for his or her favorite TV characters. Ask how your child might tell an entertaining story in a film.

Activity: At the dinner table, in the car, or elsewhere with your family, start a story. The story situation should be a real or imagined experience (for example, a difficult journey). Set up characters and a time and place. Then have each family member take turns telling what happens next.

IN THIS UNIT, YOUR CHILD WILL...

- Learn to write a story with imaginary characters and events using dialogue, descriptive details, and a clear sequence of events.

- Use linking words and phrases to signal the order of events.

- Use concrete, sensory language to tell a story precisely.

- Learn specific language skills and use them in writing a fictional narrative.

  - Use complete sentences.

  - Recognize and correct sentence fragments and run-on sentences.

  - Use commas and quotation marks when writing dialogue.

WAYS TO HELP YOUR CHILD

Encourage your child's creativity. Make telling stories a regular part of your family's activities. Invite your child to create stories and characters that interest him or her. As your child tells a story, ask for details about the characters and events. Ask why a character responds in a certain way to the story's situation. Encourage your child to use realistic dialogue and descriptive details to make the story more effective.

ONLINE
For more Home Connect activities, continue online at sadlierconnect.com

Text Types and Purposes: Write Fictional Narratives

Essential Question:
How can I write an effective story?

Write Fictional
Narratives 42

Language:
Complete Sentences 46

Language: Fragments 47

Language:
Run-on Sentences 48

Language: Commas
and Quotation Marks
in Dialogue 49

Speaking and Listening . . .50

Unit 2 Review 51

CREATING AN ORGANIZATIONAL STRUCTURE

Nicole has used a graphic organizer to organize her story. It names the story characters, shows the sequence of events, and provides a conclusion.

Title: _____

Characters: _____
_____

Story Events:

Event 1:

Event 2:

Event 3:

Event 4:

Event 5 (Conclusion):

INTRODUCTION

- Gets readers' attention
- Establishes the story situation and the main character

Underline the name of Nicole's main character. What is the story situation?

Read a Student Model

Nicole is a student in Mr. Patel's 4th-grade class. She has been asked to write a fictional narrative about someone having to move to a new place. She has been asked to use a clear sequence of events and to include dialogue and descriptive details. As you read Nicole's story, think about events and details to prepare to write your own fictional narrative.

The Longest Move

"I don't understand why we have to move," Makayla whined. "Why now?"

Makayla's father stood up from his packing and sighed. "We've talked about this, Makayla. We need to move for your mother's job, and it has to be now, not in a few years. Please finish packing. We have to load everything soon."

Makayla stomped off to her room. She was fuming over how unfair it was that she was being forced to move all the way to Mars, just because of her mother's new job as a terraforming engineer.

As she sat in her room, deciding which belongings she would take, Makayla cried. It was hard for her not to feel scared.

People had been traveling safely to Mars for 20 years, but things still could go wrong.

"And even if we survive the trip," said Makayla to her reflection in the mirror, "what about when we get there? What if I don't make any friends, or what if I hate my new school? I'll miss being able to run around outside and climb trees, too. Living on Mars is going to be awful!" Makayla nodded, and her reflection agreed.

Later, Makayla's parents came into her room to help her finish packing. Each person was allowed only 20 kilograms of cargo. Once Makayla had packed her clothes, there wasn't much room left for anything else. She chose her two favorite stuffed animals and added a poster of her favorite band. "That's something to make it look like home," she explained to her parents.

The next day, movers arrived and took the family's cargo boxes to the launch facility. Makayla sniffed a salty tear as she watched the boxes being loaded. She knew the next time she saw her belongings would be aboard the ship taking them to Mars.

Makayla's father woke her and her brother up before dawn the next morning. Their mother was waiting for them at the launch facility. When they arrived, Makayla did her best to not look scared, even though her arms tingled with goosebumps. She gave her mother a quick hug and a nervous smile.

DIALOGUE

Use dialogue to tell how characters think and feel.

In this paragraph, Nicole has Makayla talk to herself.

Put a box around Makayla's dialogue that tells what she feels she'll miss on Mars.

TRANSITIONAL WORDS AND PHRASES

Use transitional words and phrases to make the sequence of events clear. Many transitions show a change of time or place.

Underline transitional words or phrases that show a change in time.

DESCRIPTION

Use descriptive words to develop story events and characters. Sensory details help readers see, hear, feel, taste, and smell the same things the characters do.

Find and circle a sensory detail. How does the description help you understand Makayla?

WRITE FICTIONAL NARRATIVES

After the final preflight briefing, workers strapped all the passengers in for takeoff. Makayla was sitting next to a window, with her father beside her.

"I know it's scary, kiddo," he said, "but this is going to be a great adventure. Not many kids get to live on Mars for three years. And your mother and I will be there with you every step of the way. It's going to be okay—really!" He grinned and gave her a thumbs-up.

As the ship's engines roared to life, the passenger cabin began to shake. Makayla squeezed her eyes shut and gripped her father's hand.

"It's going to be okay," she whispered, over and over again.

CONCLUSION

A conclusion brings story events to an end.

Put a star next to Makayla's final thought before takeoff.

Use a graphic organizer like the one below to organize your own fictional narrative about a difficult journey. Then write a first draft of your story on a separate sheet of paper. In your draft, be sure to use dialogue and descriptions of characters' thoughts, feelings, and actions to develop your story. Also, use words and phrases to clearly show your story's events and their order. You will use this draft to write your final story draft in the Unit 2 Review section on page 52.

Title: _____

Characters: _____

_____

Story Events:

> **Event 1:**

> **Event 2:**

> **Event 3:**

> **Event 4:**

> **Event 5 (Conclusion):**

Complete Sentences

Guided Instruction A **complete sentence** includes a <u>subject</u> and a <u>verb</u>, and it expresses a complete thought. Each type of sentence begins with a capital letter and ends with a punctuation mark.

- Statement: ***Jeff** <u>watches</u>* all of our team's games.

- Question: ***Did Chandra** <u>tell</u>* you her news?

- Command: *Please **<u>read</u>** the next paragraph.* (The subject is the understood **you**.)

- Exclamation: *What a fun day **<u>we</u> <u>had</u>!***

Guided Practice Put a check mark next to each complete sentence.

_____ **1.** Suddenly ran across the street.

_____ **2.** Did Jake just hit a home run?

_____ **3.** Go to the cafeteria after school.

_____ **4.** How wonderful for you!

Independent Practice Write four of your own complete sentences, one of each type shown above. Be sure to use capital letters and the correct marks of punctuation at the end.

1. _____

_____

2. _____

_____

3. _____

_____

4. _____

_____

Fragments

Guided Instruction A **sentence fragment** is a group of words that looks like a sentence but is missing its subject or verb. Adding the missing part makes the thought complete.

Fragment	Complete Sentence
Quickly ate his breakfast. (missing subject)	**Jamal** *quickly ate his breakfast.*
The hawk above the field. (missing verb)	*The hawk* **drifted** *above the field.*

Guided Practice Write whether each group of words is a **fragment** or a **complete sentence**. If it is a fragment, write whether it is missing its **subject** or its **verb**.

1. The toddler at the new toy. *The toddler played with the new toy.*

2. Snowflakes swirled through the air. *Snoflakes flyed through the air*

3. After ten minutes of silence, spoke. *After ten minutes of silence people spoke.*

Independent Practice Correct the following fragments so that they are complete sentences.

1. Nassir soccer with his brothers.

   Nassir playes soccer with his brothers.

2. Made signs for the school concert.

   I mad signs for the concert.

3. At the sudden sound of thunder, Grace.

   At the sudden sounds of the thunder grace.

Run-on Sentences

Guided Instruction A **run-on sentence** includes too many ideas that are not properly connected. Most often, a run-on sentence occurs when two sentences are joined without proper punctuation. You can correct run-ons by adding a comma and a conjunction or by writing them as two separate sentences.

Run-on Sentence	Correction
Maria loves piano music her brothers prefer the guitar.	*Maria loves piano music,* **but** *her brothers prefer the guitar.*
Sonja's favorite class is math my favorite is English.	*Sonja's favorite class is math. My favorite is English.*

Guided Practice Draw a line between the two main thoughts in each run-on sentence.

1. Hiroshi's pet hedgehog is nocturnal it sleeps all day.

2. The bookstore was out of Volume Three it had many copies of Volume Two.

3. The day was cold and miserable we sat inside and played board games.

Independent Practice Correct the following run-on sentences.

1. Allergy season is horrible I sneeze constantly.

_____

_____

2. Luis enjoys the park he goes there almost every weekend.

_____

_____

3. Kim looked sad for a moment then she smiled.

_____

_____

Commas and Quotation Marks in Dialogue

Guided Instruction Writers use **commas and quotation marks** to set **dialogue** apart from the rest of a passage. Doing this helps readers understand who is speaking.

- *"I'm really looking forward to our class trip," said Jane.*

- *Mr. Allen replied, "The history quiz will be tomorrow."*

- *Marissa ran down the street and yelled, "Baxter! Where are you?"*

Guided Practice Add commas and quotation marks where they are needed in these sentences.

1. Please turn to page 42   said Mrs. Shore.

2. Esme looked at the mess and announced   I'm not cleaning this up.

3. From his seat in the bleachers, Peter shouted   Go, team, go!

4. Don't be late! yelled Amos.

Independent Practice Write five sentences that include dialogue. Be sure to use commas and quotation marks correctly.

1. _____

_____

2. _____

_____

3. _____

_____

4. _____

_____

5. _____

_____

Discuss the Essential Question

How can I write an effective story?

Think about the Essential Question by responding to the questions. Support your point of view with details from the story.

1. What events were in the sequence that the writer created? How did the writer make that sequence clear?

_____

_____

_____

2. What are some examples of descriptive language that the writer used?

_____

_____

Use your notes above to discuss the Essential Question in small groups or as a class. Remember to use the rules for being a good speaker and a good listener in the checklist below. When you speak, be sure to explain your ideas fully. As a listener, ask questions and make connections among everyone's comments in order to fully understand the conversation.

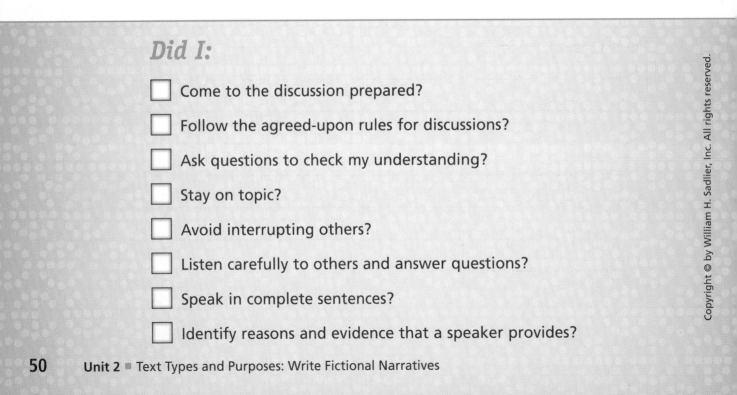

Did I:

☐ Come to the discussion prepared?

☐ Follow the agreed-upon rules for discussions?

☐ Ask questions to check my understanding?

☐ Stay on topic?

☐ Avoid interrupting others?

☐ Listen carefully to others and answer questions?

☐ Speak in complete sentences?

☐ Identify reasons and evidence that a speaker provides?

This paragraph has sentence fragments and run-on sentences. It is also missing the commas and quotation marks that set off dialogue. Write the paragraph correctly on the lines below.

The ship rose through Earth's atmosphere. Soon, reached the weightlessness of space. Makayla let go of her father's hand. The scariest part is over now he told her. Several hours after liftoff, the passengers their seat belts Makayla experienced weightlessness for the first time. Maybe three months of floating around won't be too bad she said to her parents.

Assignment: Write a fictional narrative about a difficult journey.

On the lines below, write your final copy of the fictional narrative draft you created on page 45. Be sure to present a sequence of events and to use dialogue and details to develop those events. Use descriptive words and sensory details as you describe characters and events. Use transitional words and phrases to help connect details and events, too. Then wrap up events with a conclusion. See the Writing Handbook (pages 275–283) for ways to improve your writing as you revise.

_____

_____

_____

_____

_____

_____

_____

_____

_____

_____

_____

_____

_____

_____

_____

_____

_____

_____

_____

Introducing UNIT 3

In this unit, you will learn about the earth's surface. You will explore some of the ways that changes in the earth can affect the world around us. You also will learn about natural disasters that result from changes in the earth, such as tsunamis and volcanoes. You even will learn how our planet is still changing.

In addition, you will use your skills as a critical reader to look closely at the details in nonfiction writing. You will learn to identify details and examples in a text, including those that help you draw inferences from what you are reading. You will see how key details support the main idea of a text. You will read different kinds of nonfiction writing, including scientific and technical texts, and explain their ideas and concepts based on specific information you find.

Pay close attention to the important types of information presented in each text. By the time you finish this unit, you will understand that even small changes in the earth can have big effects.

Before Unit 3

Progress Check *Can I?*

After Unit 3

	Use details to draw inferences from an informational text.	
	Determine the main idea of an informational text.	
	Summarize an informational text.	
	Explain events and ideas presented in an informational text.	
	Use affixes to determine the meaning of a word.	

HOME ◆ CONNECT...

Nonfiction authors include **examples and details** to provide text evidence for their ideas. By thinking about evidence, readers can identify what the author says directly and can **draw inferences** about what is unsaid. Help your child identify details and inferences from his or her current social studies or science textbook chapter.

The information in a nonfiction text supports a **main idea**. Children will be able to learn to identify the main idea when they **summarize** as they read. Read a nonfiction text of your child's choosing together. Pause occasionally and ask your child to summarize information. At the end, discuss the main idea of the text.

Many nonfiction texts **explain events and ideas** and their effect upon human beings. In this unit, students will read about the ways that the earth changes. Help your child understand these changes by discussing various forces of nature. Talk together about ways in which human beings are affected by our ever-changing planet.

Conversation Starter: With your child, select and discuss a news story that relates to the impact of a force of nature (for example, a hurricane, landslide, or drought). After you have read and summarized the text together, ask, "Why is this information important?" Discuss the main idea of the text as well as inferences that you might draw about the topic from the text evidence provided.

IN THIS UNIT, YOUR CHILD WILL...

- Identify details and examples that an author states in a nonfiction text and draw inferences about what the author leaves unsaid.

- Use details to determine the main idea of a text.

- Summarize a text.

- Use information in a nonfiction text to explain events and ideas.

- Use common Greek and Latin prefixes and suffixes to help define unfamiliar words.

- Compare and contrast four texts on the same theme: a procedural explanation, a scientific journal article, a scientific text, and a science magazine article.

WAYS TO HELP YOUR CHILD

Children increase their understanding of nonfiction subjects when they can make real-world connections to the subjects they read and study. Encourage your child to take an interest in history and science by showing enthusiasm for those subjects yourself (for example, by watching a TV program about a subject of interest with your child). When your child reads about a new subject, help him or her find ways to connect that information to real-life experiences.

ONLINE

For more Home Connect activities, continue online at sadlierconnect.com

Reading Informational Text: Key Ideas and Details

Essential Question:
How can readers use details to find the main idea in an informational text?

Drawing Inferences .56

Determining the Main Idea
and Summarizing .62

Explaining Events and Ideas 68

Close Reading 74

Connect Across Texts 79

Language: Affixes .80

Unit 3 Review 81

WORDS TO KNOW

erosion

formation

weathering

> Readers can use **details** and **examples** to help them understand what an author is stating directly in a text. These details and examples can also help readers draw inferences from the text.

CITE EVIDENCE

A In nonfiction writing, **details** provide the reader with information about the subject. In paragraph 1, underline three details about erosion.

B Details can help readers understand the steps in a process. Put a box around the details that explain the first step in erosion by water. What details are in the next step?

Erosion and Earth's Changing Landscape

(Genre: Explanatory Text/Procedural)

1   Have you ever looked at a muddy river and wondered how it became so dirty? The answer is **erosion**, the process through which soil is moved. Natural forces cause much of the erosion in the environment, but people contribute to it, too. Erosion sometimes creates amazing natural wonders, such as the Grand Canyon in Arizona. Often, though, erosion is simply harmful to the environment.

Erosion by Water

2   The most common type of erosion is erosion by water. Water moves dirt and rocks through the landscape, causing changes in Earth's surface. Erosion by water happens in three basic steps:

- **Weathering**, or the weakening of solid rock through weather and age, breaks down larger rock **formations**. The larger rocks are turned into dirt and pebbles.
- Rain falls and flows across the landscape. The rain carries the dirt and smaller rocks that were broken down through weathering.
- The rainfall causes small streams and rivers to flow. This moving water wears away the banks of the river, widening the river valley.

Guided Instruction

3   Ocean waves have a similar effect on coastlines. The powerful waves move against the shoreline, pushing the sand of the beaches farther back.

4   The Grand Canyon is an unforgettable example of the effects of erosion by water. Long ago, rainfall caused the Colorado River to move over the desert floor with great power. The rain weathered the solid rock. Over time, the Colorado River carved out a canyon that is almost 300 miles long, 18 miles across, and—in places—more than a mile deep.

5   You can see another effect of erosion by water at the Cape Hatteras Lighthouse in North Carolina. The lighthouse was built in 1870. It was placed on the beach, 3,300 feet away from the ocean. Over the years, the ocean has eroded the beach. By 1999, the lighthouse was sitting on the shoreline. People were afraid that a large storm could cause the structure to collapse. Eventually, the lighthouse was moved back. It now sits 2,900 feet away from the ocean.

CITE EVIDENCE

C **Examples** can provide evidence, or proof, of an author's ideas. This author presents specific examples in paragraphs 4 and 5. Circle the names of the places that provide evidence in the form of an example.

D You can use details to **draw inferences**—that is, to form your own ideas. In paragraph 4, underline details about the size of the Grand Canyon. What inference might you draw from those details?

Comprehension Check

What can you infer about the power of nature from the details and examples in the text? Support your answer with specific text evidence.

Grand Canyon

DRAWING INFERENCES

Erosion and Earth's Changing Landscape *continued*

WORDS TO KNOW

basin

glacier

particle

sediment

CITE EVIDENCE

A In paragraph 6, circle the example that the author uses to illustrate the effects of erosion by ice. Circle the specific example that illustrates wind erosion in paragraph 8.

B In paragraph 7, underline the details that tell about the effects of wind erosion. What inference can you draw from these details?

Erosion by Ice

6   Erosion by ice is a direct effect of the movement of **glaciers**. Glaciers are large mountains of ice and rock. In cold areas, glaciers move across the land. Moving glaciers pick up dirt and **sediment**, which scrape across the land and wear away at the ground. As the ground breaks down under the glacier, valleys and river **basins** are created. One example of erosion by ice is the Finger Lakes area of New York. When a glacier eroded the landscape, it created large basins that filled with water and became the Finger Lakes.

Erosion by Wind

7   Wind is another cause of erosion. As wind blows across the land, it picks up **particles**, or very small pieces, of sand and soil and moves them to different locations. Some particles contribute to the creation of new natural formations. But particles can also wear away existing landforms. Here's how:

- As wind blows, it picks up small particles of dirt and sand.
- Sometimes, the dirt and sand are blown into large piles, creating sand dunes.
- At other times, the wind blows against the rock faces of mountains and other formations. Particles of dirt and sand act like a sandblaster, smoothing and eroding the rock and changing its structure.

8   Arches National Park, in Utah, is a natural structure formed by wind erosion. The wind blew against the rock faces for a very long time, smoothing them. The only parts of the rock left behind were naturally occurring arches.

9   There are more than 2,000 arches located in the park. The largest arch, Landscape Arch, is 306 feet long from base to base. Imagine the power it took to create a 306-foot-long arch! Even today, the harsh winds of the Utah desert erode the rocks, and the shapes of the arches change. Who knows what the arches will look like 1,000 or 100,000 years from now?

Comprehension Check

1. Think about the details you have read. Which process created the Finger Lakes?

   a. erosion by wind

   b. erosion by humans

   c. erosion by water

   d. erosion by ice

2. From the evidence in paragraphs 7–9, you can infer that

   a. wind erosion causes more damage than water erosion does.

   b. over time, wind erosion could completely wear away a rock.

   c. sand dunes never occur near mountains.

   d. you can find more wind erosion in Utah than anywhere else.

3. With a partner, draw an inference based on the text about which is more dangerous for humans—water erosion or wind erosion. Explain.

_____

_____

_____

_____

DRAWING INFERENCES

Independent Practice

Erosion and Earth's Changing Landscape *continued*

WORDS TO KNOW

demonstrate

deteriorate

permanent

CITE EVIDENCE

A Put a star by the section that contains a procedural, or "how to," activity. What inference can you draw about the reason the author included this procedure?

B Underline the details in paragraph 14 that directly, or explicitly, state the author's purpose in presenting the information in paragraphs 10–13.

Erosion by Humans

10   Human activities contribute to land erosion, too. People cut down trees and remove other plants to make room for buildings and farmland. This is a problem, for the roots of trees and plants hold the soil in place. When people remove trees and plants, the land **deteriorates**. Flooding, landslides, and mudslides result.

11   Something can be done about this kind of erosion, however. People can plant trees and other plants to prevent a water source, such as rain or a flood, from washing land away.

12   You and a partner can make a model that shows how plants help slow down or even stop soil erosion.

- First, get two large, deep rectangular glass baking dishes.
- Fill one dish with regular soil from your area and the other with a small rectangular patch of sod, or grass-covered soil (also called turf).
- Now blow hard on the tray with soil. You might even try aiming a small fan at it. Do you see any dirt particles fly out?
- Blow on the tray with sod. Do any soil particles blow off?
- Next, hold the dish with the soil at an angle. Have your partner pour some water onto the soil. How does the water act on the soil?
- Now repeat the process with the dish that has sod in it. Does the water move the soil this time?

Tree roots can hold in soil and lessen soil erosion.

7　　Most volcanoes develop at the boundaries of two tectonic plates. Tectonic plates separate and collide, creating cracks in Earth's crust. Magma is able to push through these cracks to become lava. Some volcanoes form at hot spots, or weak places in the crust. The volcanoes in the Hawaiian Islands often form at hot spots.

8　　There are four main types of volcanoes: shield volcanoes, cinder cone volcanoes, lava dome volcanoes, and composite volcanoes. Scientists classify volcanoes based on their shape and on the type of lava they produce.

9　　The largest volcanoes in the world are shield volcanoes. Shield volcanoes form from rapidly flowing lava. The lava cools and creates a dome shape. Some shield volcanoes overlap with others. The Big Island of Hawaii is actually made up of five shield volcanoes.

10　　Cinder cone volcanoes are the most common type of volcano. Cinder cone volcanoes erupt with violent explosions. The eruptions push lava into the air. When the lava cools, it forms the sides of the volcano. Cinder

11　　A lava dome is a round volcano. It forms when sticky lava flows slowly over the landscape. Sometimes, lava domes can be created after an explosive eruption. All of the gas insid the volcano is released. All that is left i the slow-moving lava. The lava builds up in a round dome shape.

12　　A composite volcano usually looks like a tall mountain before it erupts. The gas inside the volcano builds up and causes an explosive eruption. Sometimes, it looks as if the whole top of the mountain has blown off. Mount St. Helens is a composite volcano.

13　　Volcanoes can be either active or dormant. Active volcanoes are those that have erupted sometime in the past 10,000 years. Dormant volcanoes have been quiet for a long time but may

14   Just as there are different types of volcanoes, there are different types of eruptions. Volcanic eruptions are named after the region in which they are found. For example, Hawaiian eruptions are gentle, with quickly moving lava flows. In Strombolian eruptions, lava spurts into the air repeatedly. Plinian eruptions are explosive eruptions of ash and steam.

15   There are at least 50 active volcanoes in the United States. These volcanoes are expected to erupt again. Most of these volcanoes are part of the large group of active volcanoes that circle the Pacific Ocean. This group is called the Ring of Fire. More than 75% of the world's active volcanoes are part of

16   Volcanoes in North America are of all types. They display different kinds of eruptions. Some of the best-known volcanoes are in Hawaii, in the Pacific Northwest, and in Alaska.

17   Kilauea, a shield volcano, is the youngest volcano on the Big Island of Hawaii. Many scientists believe that Kilauea began to form sometime between 300,000 and 600,000 years ago. It has been erupting ever since. Scientists study Kilauea to learn more about active volcanoes.

18   Sunset Crater Volcano National Monument, in Arizona, is a dormant cinder cone volcano. It erupted in the year 1065, but scientists believe that

19   The area around Sunset Crater is covered in volcanic rock. The mountain is made of a thick blanket of cinders. Visitors to the monument have a difficult time walking in the cinder deposits. In other areas, the landscape has large, sharp pieces of cooled lava. Visitors can take a tour of the volcano and learn about other cinder cones in North America.

20   Mount St. Helens may be the best-known volcano in the United States. This active volcano is located in the western Cascade Mountains of Washington. It was once a majestic mountain with a snow-capped peak. Now, it is best known for its explosive eruption in 1980.

21   Mount St. Helens was releasing steam and ash for two months before the first eruption occurred on May 18, 1980. The explosion blew off one side of the mountain, reshaping its appearance. It destroyed forests and wildlife. On May 25, a second eruption created a lava dome in the crater of the first eruption.

22   Volcanoes are destructive, but they also are rich in minerals and precious gems. In addition, the soil that eventually develops from volcanic eruptions often leads to better plant and animal life. As scientists continue to study volcanoes, they learn more about how these powerful giants behave.

Comprehension Check

1. From text evidence in paragraphs 1–3 and 20–21, you can infer that Mount St. Helens

    a. is not in the Ring of Fire.

    b. changed appearance drastically and quickly.

    c. is a cinder cone volcano.

    d. has now gone extinct after erupting in 1980.

2. Which sentence from page 74 expresses the main idea of this article?

    a. This is exactly what happened when Mount St. Helens erupted in 1980.

    b. Few of us have seen an erupting volcano.

    c. There are many active and dormant volcanoes in North America today.

    d. When magma reaches the surface, it becomes lava.

3. your own words, summarize the events in paragraph 6 that explain ow a volcano forms.

_____

_____

_____

_____

_____

_____

_____

_____

4. Think about what you have just read. Where are most of the volcanoes in North America located, and why there? Use details from the article to provide evidence for your answer.

_____

_____

_____

_____

_____

_____

_____

_____

Compare and Contrast Texts

In this unit, you read four texts that describe forces that change Earth's surface. Think about the different ways that these forces were explained. Then choose two of the texts and compare and contrast them using the T-chart below. Write the titles of the texts you chose in the top row. List important details to show how the texts are similar or different underneath. Be prepared to discuss your ideas with your class.

Return to the Essential Question

How can readers use details to find the main idea in an informational text?

In a small group or as a class, discuss the Essential Question. Think about what you have learned about main ideas and text evidence; about drawing inferences and explaining events and ideas; and about summarizing. Use evidence from the four unit texts to answer the question.

Affixes

Guided Instruction An **affix** is a word part that can be attached to the beginning or end of a root or base word. You often can determine the meanings of words with affixes by dividing them into their parts. For example, in *prefix, pre-* means "before" and *fix* means "to attach." So, a *prefix* is an affix that is *attached before* the root or base word. A **suffix** is attached after the root or base word. *Adaptable*, for example, is the base *adapt* with the suffix *-able*. The word means "having the ability to adapt."

Affix	Meaning
pre- (prefix)	before
re- (prefix)	again
-ful (suffix)	full of
-ous (suffix)	having
-able (suffix)	having an ability

Guided Practice Use the chart of affixes to determine the meaning of the words in **bold type** below (from "The Power of Tsunamis").

1. The **courageous** people who live where tsunamis occur must keep aware of the ocean's movements.

_____

2. The flooding washed away more than 125,000 buildings, and **rebuilding** will take years.

_____

Independent Practice Use affixes and base words to figure out the meanings of these words from "Volcanoes: Nature's Fire." Then write a sentence of your own for each of them.

3. beautiful (paragraph 1) _____

_____

4. reshaping (paragraph 21) _____

_____

Read the following science article. Pay attention to the details in the article that help you understand the author's ideas. Then answer the questions on pages 81 and 82.

Recording an Earthquake

(Genre: Scientific Journal Article)

1   More than 100,000 earthquakes occur every year. Most are small underground vibrations. Only about 1,000 earthquakes are strong enough to reshape the earth. So, then, how do scientists know that an earthquake has occurred?

2   Scientists measure earthquakes with a *seismograph*, an instrument that records underground movements.

When the earth moves underneath a seismograph, the movement creates an electrical current. The electricity moves a light beam across a sheet of photographic paper. The light beam draws a line. The line spikes higher as the vibrations get stronger. Higher spikes show powerful earthquakes. Lower spikes show normal movement. In this way, scientists can record every time an earthquake occurs.

Fill in the circle of the correct answer choice.

1. What is one detail about earthquakes that appears in paragraph 1?

   ○ Electricity moves a light beam.

   ○ Earthquakes happen along the San Andreas Fault.

   ○ Tectonic plates shift and collide.

   ○ About 100,000 earthquakes happen each year.

2. In paragraph 2, the author explains that a *seismograph* is

   ○ an instrument to measure earthquakes.

   ○ an effect of shifting plates.

   ○ a tool to create underground vibrations.

   ○ a tool to prevent earthquakes.

3. What does the word *recordable* mean?

    ○ full of records   ○ able to be recorded

    ○ to record again   ○ to record beforehand

4. To *reshape* something is to

    ○ shape it beforehand.   ○ have some kind of shape.

    ○ have a full shape.   ○ shape it again.

5. What can you infer from the fact that the author not only defines *seismograph* but also explains how a seismograph works?

_____

_____

6. In paragraph 2, underline the sentence that best illustrates the main idea of the article.

7. List the events that occur when a seismograph records movements in the earth.

_____

_____

8. Use details in the text to explain the spikes in a seismographic record.

_____

9. What text evidence supports the idea that only a small percentage of earthquakes are dangerous?

_____

_____

10. Summarize this article in two sentences.

_____

_____

_____

Introducing UNIT 4

Weather changes, seasons change, and the earth itself changes. What do you know about these kinds of changes? How might you share what you know with others? In this unit about ways in which nature can change the earth, you will learn how to write an informative/explanatory text.

When you do this kind of writing, you examine a topic and share ideas and information about it. For example, you might write about the causes and effects of an earthquake or the aftermath of a volcanic explosion. Whatever the topic, you develop your ideas with supporting facts, definitions, and details.

An effective informative/explanatory text is well organized. The writing should include precise words to be accurate and interesting, and it should be grammatically correct.

Before Unit 4

Progress Check *Can I?*

After Unit 4

☐ ☐ Organize an informative/explanatory text with an introduction, subtopics, and a conclusion.

☐ ☐ Use facts, definitions, and details to support ideas.

☐ ☐ Use linking words to connect ideas.

☐ ☐ Write using prepositional phrases correctly.

☐ ☐ Write using progressive verb forms.

☐ ☐ Write using precise words and phrases.

☐ ☐ Write using the correct order of adjectives.

HOME◆CONNECT...

- Learn to write an informative or explanatory piece that introduces a topic, groups related information, and ends with a conclusion.

- Use facts, definitions, and details to support the topic.

- Learn to use linking words, such as *also, another, for example,* and *because*, to connect ideas.

- Use precise language and subject vocabulary to explain the topic.

- Learn specific language skills and use them in writing an informative or explanatory piece:

  - Use prepositional phrases.

  - Use progressive verbs.

  - Choose words and phrases that convey ideas precisely.

  - Use adjectives in the correct order.

In this unit, children will learn about writing to present information about a topic or to explain a process. Help your child identify **informative/explanatory texts** in the world around you, including magazine and website articles, biographies, cookbooks, and travel guides.

Have your child select a favorite nonfiction book. Model identifying how the author **introduces and develops the topic**. Discuss how the author **organizes information and makes the information clear** to readers. Challenge your child to talk about what he or she would say if writing about the same topic or a similar topic.

Ask your child to think about a topic that he or she knows well. Have your child write down **facts and details** that he or she already knows about the topic. Discuss how he or she would write about the topic (for example, in a magazine article? an Internet blog?) and what he or she might do to help make the information or explanation clear.

On The Go: When your child expresses interest in a topic (for example, one of the topics in this unit is about changes in the earth), help him or her to locate and read a print or online informative/explanatory text about it. Encourage your child to write and share a paragraph that presents information or an explanation of something covered in that text.

WAYS TO HELP YOUR CHILD

Help your child develop patience with the writing process. Remind your child that informative/explanatory writing includes gathering information, organizing it, writing a draft, editing it, and creating a final version. Emphasize that all of these steps are important.

ONLINE

For more Home Connect activities, continue online at sadlierconnect.com

Text Types and Purposes: Write Informative/ Explanatory Texts

UNIT **4**

Essential Question:
How can I explain a topic in writing?

Write Informative/
Explanatory Texts 86

Language:
Prepositional Phrases. 90

Language: Progressive Forms
of Verbs 91

Language: Precise Words
and Phrases. 92

Language: Order
of Adjectives 93

Speaking and Listening. . .94

Unit 4 Review 95

CREATING AN ORGANIZATIONAL STRUCTURE

Shana has used an outline to organize her explanatory essay. It has an introduction to the main topic, three subtopics, and a conclusion.

Title: _____

I. Introduction
   a. Topic: _____
   b. Background: _____

II. Subtopic 1: _____
   Fact/Detail: _____

III. Subtopic 2: _____
   Fact/Detail: _____

IV. Subtopic 3: _____
   Fact/Detail: _____

V. Conclusion
   _____
   _____
   _____

TITLE

Identifies the main topic for the reader

INTRODUCTION

- Gets the reader's attention
- Introduces the main topic
- Gives background
- States what the writer will examine

Underline the sentence that states what Shana will examine about the topic.

Read a Student Model

Shana is a student in Mr. Moreno's 4th-grade class. She has been asked to write an informative/explanatory text about how a natural phenomenon can change the earth. She has been asked to develop her main topic with three subtopics. As you read Shana's explanatory essay, think about a topic, subtopics, and type of organization to prepare to write your own informative/ explanatory text.

October 29, 2012

October 27, 2012

Hurricane Sandy and the Mid-Atlantic Region

Imagine waking up to find your house or street covered in sand. That's what happened to some people after Hurricane Sandy tore through the mid-Atlantic states on October 29, 2012. When it hit New Jersey, it was just a category 1 hurricane. That's the lowest level. However, it was the largest Atlantic storm ever. It stretched for 900 miles. Hurricane Sandy's wide path of winds pushed ocean water toward the coast. This caused a storm surge, or a rise in sea level. The water rose 14 feet in some places. When it hit land, the storm surge changed the coastlines of Maryland, Delaware, New Jersey, and New York in three big ways.

Eroded Beaches

One way Hurricane Sandy's storm surge changed the coastline was by eroding beaches. The rushing water swept sand from the beaches inland. Streets and backyards were covered with sand. Some people even found sand in their basements. This movement of sand made the beaches narrower. Some beaches are 40 feet narrower now because of Hurricane Sandy.

Damaged Barrier Islands

Another way the storm surge changed the coastline was by damaging barrier islands. A barrier island is a long, narrow island that runs along a coast. Just as with the beaches, the storm surge eroded many of the barrier islands. It carried sand from the islands all the way to coastal inlands. The storm surge carried half a million cubic yards of sand from just one island.

Destroyed Dunes

A third way Hurriane Sandy changed the coastline was by destroying dunes. A dune is a mound of sand. Dunes form on coastal beaches and barrier islands. The powerful storm surge washed many dunes away. Local officials have put more than 3,000 old Christmas trees on their beaches. They hope that blowing sand will build up on the trees and replace missing dunes.

HEADINGS

Use headings to indicate different sections, or subtopics. Be sure to use precise language to make the information clear.

SUBTOPIC 1:

Group information about one subtopic into each section.

Shana develops her subtopics with facts, definitions, and details. She chooses words and phrases to link information in each subtopic.

SUBTOPIC 2:

Underline the sentence that states Shana's second subtopic.

Put a box around one fact she includes to develop this subtopic.

SUBTOPIC 3:

Underline the sentence that states Shana's third subtopic.

Circle a definition that Shana includes.

WRITE INFORMATIVE/EXPLANATORY TEXTS

Hurricane Sandy had a huge impact on the mid-Atlantic coastline. The hurricane's storm surge changed the natural landscape. It eroded beaches and barrier islands. It also washed away dunes. Before-and-after photographs of the coastline make the changes clear.

What the photographs do not show is that the area is now at greater risk during future hurricanes. Future storm surges will have a shorter distance to travel over beaches to reach inland. They also will encounter smaller and fewer barrier islands and dunes. These act as walls against rising waters.

The damage from Hurricane Sandy was great. However, it could be even worse in the future because of the changes to the coastline.

CONCLUSION

Shana's conclusion restates her opening statement in slightly different words. It wraps up her explanation of the topic and provides an interesting thought about it.

Underline the two sentences that form the conclusion of Shana's explanatory essay.

May 21, 2009

Before Hurricane Sandy

November 5, 2012

After Hurricane Sandy

Use an outline to organize your informative/explanatory essay about a natural phenomenon that changes the earth. Then write a first draft on a separate piece of paper. Be sure to introduce your topic and develop it with facts and details. Use precise words to explain the topic. Connect your ideas with linking words or phrases, and end with a concluding statement. You will use this draft to write your final article in the Unit 4 Review section on page 96.

Title: _____

I. Introduction

   a. Topic: _____

   b. Background: _____

   _____

II. Subtopic 1: _____

   Fact/Detail: _____

   _____

III. Subtopic 2: _____

   Fact/Detail: _____

   _____

IV. Subtopic 3: _____

   Fact/Detail: _____

   _____

V. Conclusion

   _____

   _____

   _____

Prepositional Phrases

Guided Instruction A **prepositional phrase** begins with a preposition and ends with a noun or pronoun. A prepositional phrase tells *when, where,* or *how* something happens.

Some prepositional phrases include a preposition and a noun or pronoun.

> *Ramón ate lunch* **with Elsa**. *(with* = preposition; *Elsa* = noun*)*
> *Cassie talked* **to her** *later. (to* = preposition; *her* = pronoun*)*

Other prepositional phrases include a preposition, a modifier, and a noun.

> **In the afternoon**, *Marco and his sister will rake the yard.*
> *(In* = preposition; *the* = modifier; *afternoon* = noun*)*
> *Alexis puts the books* **on those metal shelves**.
> *(on* = preposition; *those, metal* = modifiers; *shelves* = noun*)*

Guided Practice Complete the sentences with prepositional phrases. Use the prepositions in parentheses.

1. I put my little brother's toys (into) _____.

2. That dog just barked (at) _____.

3. (After) _____, Ben and his mom went (to) _____.

Independent Practice Write four of your own sentences. In the first three sentences, use one prepositional phrase. In the fourth sentence, use two prepositional phrases.

1. _____

_____

2. _____

_____

3. _____

_____

4. _____

_____

Progressive Forms of Verbs

Guided Instruction The **progressive forms of verbs** show that action keeps on going.

- The **present progressive** form uses *am/is/are* + a verb + *ing*.

  *I **am walking**. He **is walking**. They **are walking**.*

- The **past progressive** form uses *was/were* + a verb + *ing*.

  *I **was walking**. You **were walking**.*

- The **future progressive** form uses *will* + a verb + *ing*.

  *I **will be walking**. We **will be walking**.*

Guided Practice Complete each sentence using the correct progressive form of the verb *to study*.

1. Today, Takira _____ in class.

2. Yesterday, Takira _____ with me.

3. Tomorrow, Takira _____ at home.

Independent Practice Write four sentences of your own. Use the present progressive form of a verb in the first sentence, the past progressive form in the second, and the future progressive in the third. In the fourth sentence, for an extra challenge, use verbs in two progressive forms.

1. _____

_____

2. _____

_____

3. _____

_____

4. _____

_____

Precise Words and Phrases

Guided Instruction **Precise words and phrases** help make writing clear and vivid. They can signal precise actions, emotions, or states of being.

Unclear and Uninteresting	Precise and Vivid
The food was good.	*The **spaghetti** was **delicious**.*
The animal went somewhere.	*The **puppy squeezed under the bed**.*

Guided Practice Replace each unclear and uninteresting word or phrase in parentheses with a precise word or phrase from the Word Bank.

Word Bank		
blanketed	clang	dusted
expert on hurricanes	guest speaker	squeak

1. The old bicycle tires (make a noise) _____.

2. The snow (covered) _____ the ground.

3. We will ask the (person) _____ many questions.

Independent Practice Write three of your own sentences using precise words and phrases.

1. _____

_____

2. _____

_____

3. _____

_____

Order of Adjectives

Guided Instruction When you use more than one **adjective** to describe something, think about the correct **order**.

Order of Adjectives								
Number	Opinion	Size	Age	Shape	Color	Origin	Material	Purpose
two *many*	*nice* *scary*	*tiny* *big*	*young* *old*	*round* *square*	*blue* *green*	*American* *Chinese*	*paper* *cotton*	*grocery (bag)* *summer (jacket)*

- INCORRECT: *The restaurant serves* **Indian delicious** *food.*
  CORRECT: *The restaurant serves* **delicious Indian** *food.* (opinion, origin)

- INCORRECT: *Kylie left her* **cool running new** *shoes at home.*
  CORRECT: *Kylie left her* **cool new running** *shoes at home.* (opinion, age, purpose)

Guided Practice Complete each sentence with the correct order of adjectives.

1. Caleb bought _____ caps. (baseball, two)

2. We live near _____ farms. (huge, old, several)

3. Do you have any _____ frames? (picture, silver, square)

Independent Practice Write three of your own sentences. In each sentence, use at least two adjectives in the correct order.

1. _____

_____

2. _____

_____

3. _____

_____

Discuss the Essential Question

How can I explain a topic in writing?

Think about the Essential Question by responding to the questions below. Support your point of view with facts and details from the article.

1. What topic did the writer explain?

_____

_____

2. What subtopics and facts did the writer include to develop the main topic?

_____

_____

_____

_____

Use your notes above to discuss the Essential Question in small groups or as a class. Follow agreed-upon rules of discussion. Use the organizer below to record what you heard and how you participated. Remember to identify reasons and evidence provided by different speakers in your discussion.

Ideas I Agree or Disagree With		Questions I Asked
Agree		
Disagree		
New Ideas I Had During Discussion		Questions I Answered

This paragraph has mistakes in prepositional phrases, the progressive forms of verbs, the use of precise words, and the order of adjectives. Write the paragraph correctly on the lines below.

Mount St. Helens is a volcano in the state Washington. It erupted in 1980. An earthquake triggered the eruption. Tons of volcanic gray ash went into the air. Heat from the blast melted glaciers on the volcano. The eruption was so bad that the north side of the volcano slid into the valley. Forests burned down, and rivers flooded the surrounding land. Mount St. Helens is active today. Years from now, scientists still do research with it.

_____

_____

_____

_____

_____

_____

_____

_____

_____

_____

_____

_____

_____

Assignment: Write an informative/explanatory essay about a natural phenomenon that changes the earth.

On the lines below, write your final copy of the informative/explanatory essay draft you created on page 89. Be sure to tell what natural phenomenon you are examining and to develop your topic with subtopics and facts, definitions, and details. Use precise language, and include a conclusion that summarizes the information you present. See the Writing Handbook (pages 275–283) for ways to improve your writing as you revise.

_____

_____

_____

_____

_____

_____

_____

_____

_____

_____

_____

_____

_____

_____

_____

_____

_____

_____

_____

Introducing UNIT 5

Think about the stories that you enjoy the most, and why you enjoy them. You probably like to read about interesting characters doing exciting things. In this unit, you'll read about brave people and their bold adventures. Authors work hard to tell those kinds of stories. How do they figure out the best way to tell their stories?

One thing authors do is to choose a structure for their stories. In this unit, you will read some traditional stories, but that's not all. You will see that poems, plays, letters, and journal entries can tell stories, too. Authors also create exciting stories by using their craft—their skill in making writing interesting. In this unit, you will learn how word choices, point of view, and figurative language can make a story fun to read and easy to remember.

Progress Check *Can I?*

Before Unit 5		After Unit 5
☐	Figure out what words and phrases in a text mean.	☐
☐	Explain the main differences between poetry, drama, and prose.	☐
☐	Refer to the features of poetry (such as verse and rhythm) or drama (such as dialogue and stage directions) when I write or talk about a text.	☐
☐	Compare and contrast the points of view in different stories.	☐
☐	Explain the difference between first-person and third-person points of view.	☐
☐	Understand similes and metaphors in a piece of writing.	☐

HOME ◆ CONNECT...

- Understand the meanings of words and phrases that come from mythology.

- Identify the differences between poems, plays, and prose.

- Learn about structural features of plays, such as casts of characters, dialogue, and stage directions.

- Compare and contrast the points of view from which different stories are narrated.

- Explain the meanings of similes and metaphors in a particular context.

- Compare and contrast four texts on the same theme: a realistic fiction story, an historical drama, an historical fiction story, and a series of journal entries.

Stories sometimes include **words that come from characters in mythology**. Choose one of these words: *tantalize, echo, narcissistic,* or *herculean.* Locate the corresponding myth and read it with your child. Discuss how the meaning of the word is related to the myth.

Drama has **structural elements**, such as casts of characters, dialogue, and stage directions. With your child, write a short play about an experience you shared. Cast family members in the play and perform it together.

Stories are narrated, or told, from different points of view. A first-person narrator is a character in the story who tells the story using *I.* A third-person narrator is someone who is outside the story and tells the story using *he* or *she.* Choose a story that you and your child enjoy. Decide whether it is told by a first-person narrator or a third-person narrator. Then retell it from the other point of view. **Compare and contrast the points of view**.

WAYS TO HELP YOUR CHILD

Help your child develop thinking and speaking skills by asking him or her to tell stories about real-life events or to retell stories from a book, TV show, or movie. Ask questions that encourage your child to include details and to think about the perspective of those who are involved in the event or story.

Activity: With your child, conduct a Web search for the painting *Washington Crossing the Delaware.* Take turns telling a story about what you think is happening in the painting. Then, read about the brave, bold event that the painting portrays. Discuss what you might include if you wrote a first-person account, a third-person account, a poem, or a play about the event shown in the painting.

ONLINE

For more Home Connect activities, continue online at sadlierconnect.com

14   On the day they left to return to Mount Vernon, there was a letter waiting for Aunt Martha. She asked Polly to read it aloud.

15   *Dear Lady Washington,*

   Last Thanksgiving, when all we had was a scoop of rice, I wasn't sure we would last the winter or ever be able to fight the British. Three people changed all that. Your great husband and Baron von Steuben taught us to be a real army. But you helped us survive to become one, and you brought us hope again. Thank you.

   Your servant, Robert Finney

Comprehension Check   MORE ONLINE   sadlierconnect.com

1. What is the point of view in paragraph 12?

   a. first person

   b. third person

   c. both first person and third person

   d. neither first person nor third person

2. Which word in paragraph 15 shows that the paragraph has a first-person point of view?

   a. Lady Washington

   b. us

   c. you

   d. your

3. Most parts of "Bringing Hope to the Valley" are told by an outside narrator. A few parts are told by a character in the story. How do the different points of view help you understand this story?

_____

_____

_____

James Armistead:
Spying for the Revolution
(Genre: Journal Entries)

Journal Entry 1

1 Last year, in third grade, we studied our family trees. I found out that an ancestor of mine was a famous spy! No, I'm not a descendant of James Bond. But my ancestor is just as cool as Bond—cooler, actually, because he was a real person who had a great effect on American history.

2 My ancestor, James Armistead, is a hero of the American Revolution. But hardly anyone has ever heard of him, and that's ridiculous! Without his work as a spy, we Americans might not have won the Revolutionary War. There might not even be a United States as we know it today. I want to tell everyone about my ancestor. He should be a hero to all Americans!

3 James Armistead spied for the Americans while pretending to spy for the British. He was a double agent! He must have been very clever to find the information he needed, and very brave to keep his true loyalties a secret from the British. He must have had to live constantly with the fear of being discovered by the British.

4 Armistead learned important facts about the British army that helped the Americans win the Revolutionary War. After the war, though, he had to return to a life of enslavement. That would have made me furious! He helped bring Americans freedom, but then he was sent back to be treated like property and was not allowed to have freedom himself. Liberty must have seemed like a dream that would never come true for him.

5 Why is James Armistead my hero? It's not just because he fought bravely for our country. It's because he risked his life for the benefit of others, and he didn't get anything out of it. There was no reward for him. When I think of him, I think of the proverb "Virtue is its own reward." Armistead's actions show the kind of behavior that my mom calls "altruism." Altruism means doing the right thing for others, even if they don't know you're doing it, and even if you get no thanks for doing it. My mom says we should all try to live like that—doing what's right, just because it's right.

6 I also think James Armistead is great because he helped win the war in a way that didn't involve violence. Instead, he spied on the British and gave them false information. He helped win the war by learning about the British troop movements. I'm really impressed by how he used information and intelligence instead of force.

Journal Entry 2

7 I asked everyone I know if they'd heard of James Armistead. Absolutely no one had! I want to let all of my friends know about him and how important he was to our country. I am writing an article for the school paper about him and why we should all know who he is. Here's my first draft.

A Forgotten Hero

8 James Armistead was born an enslaved person in Virginia. As a teenager, he volunteered to help in the Revolutionary War as a spy. Many black people, both enslaved and free, were part of the Revolutionary War. Some were soldiers, and others, like James Armistead, were spies.

9 Armistead was not an average spy, though. He was a double agent, who pretended to spy *for* the British while really spying *on* them and giving them false information. Some of the information he gained from the British helped the Americans win the war.

10 James Armistead worked for the Marquis de Lafayette, a young French general who had also volunteered to help the Americans. The American troops were inexperienced, and Lafayette needed help to fight the British army.

11   Armistead's job was to get that help by acting as a spy. He pretended to have escaped enslavement and joined the British camp of General Cornwallis. But the British recruited him to spy for them, too! Armistead passed on important information to other American spies. He also started giving the British false information. He tricked them into thinking that the American army was stronger than it really was.

12   The British shared their plans and strategies with Armistead. One day, he learned that the British were planning to move about 10,000 soldiers to Yorktown, Virginia, on ships. Using this information, French forces under the command of Lafayette, combined with American forces under the command of George Washington, surrounded Yorktown. They forced the British troops to surrender—and won the war!

13   The American victory would not have been possible without Armistead and his work as a double agent. But after the war, James Armistead was sent back to his life of enslavement. He had just been involved in exciting and important work, with people who treated him as an equal. He had put his life on the line, since every time he had encounters with the British he was in danger of being discovered as a spy. His life could not have been easy, but he probably felt proud of his role as a double agent. To lose all of that by going back to life as an enslaved person would have been very hard on him.

14   Fortunately, the Marquis de Lafayette helped Armistead gain his freedom a few years later. Armistead took the last name "Lafayette" in gratitude. He had a family and lived as a farmer in Virginia until his death in 1830.

15   Today, although all Americans know about Revolutionary War figures like George Washington, Patrick Henry, and John Adams, Armistead is almost unknown. Since his spy work led directly to the American victory over the British, all Americans today should know his name and thank him for helping to give our country its independence!

Journal Entry 3

16   My English teacher saw the article I'm working on for the next issue of the school newspaper. She asked me to write a poem about James Armistead for the Heroes Wall in our classroom. Here's my poem!

Remembering James Armistead

17   *James Armistead believed in liberty,*
The tantalizing dream of freedom
That called Americans to rebel
*   against rules.*

18   *James Armistead heard the call.*
He volunteered to help the country
That had kept him enslaved.

19   *James Armistead used his mind.*
He listened, spied, and tricked,
Finding the clues to win the war.

20   *He fought for our liberty.*
He must never be forgotten.

Comprehension Check

1. Use clues in paragraph 5 to figure out what *altruism* means. Circle the letter of the correct definition.

   a. loving your country

   b. volunteering to do a good thing

   c. risking your life to help other people

   d. doing the right thing for no reward

2. In Greek mythology, the Furies were three winged goddesses who would go after wrongdoers and drive them to madness. Which word in paragraph 4 comes from their name?

   a. furious

   b. liberty

   c. freedom

   d. dream

3. Think about the different ways that the writer speaks about James Armistead in journal entries 1 and 2. What point of view does she use in each entry? What information about James Armistead does she share in each entry? Give examples.

_____

_____

_____

_____

_____

_____

_____

_____

4. The writer uses two different forms as she writes in her journal. Name the forms and then explain how you recognized each form. Use details from the text to explain your answer.

_____

_____

_____

_____

_____

_____

_____

_____

Compare and Contrast Texts

In this unit, you read about Paul Revere's midnight ride, the Battles of Saratoga, Martha Washington's visit to Valley Forge, and Revolutionary War spy James Armistead. Each of these stories was told in a different way. Pick two texts and describe how they were told and what you learned about the Revolutionary War from them. How did the way the story was told affect what you learned? Be prepared to discuss your ideas with your class.

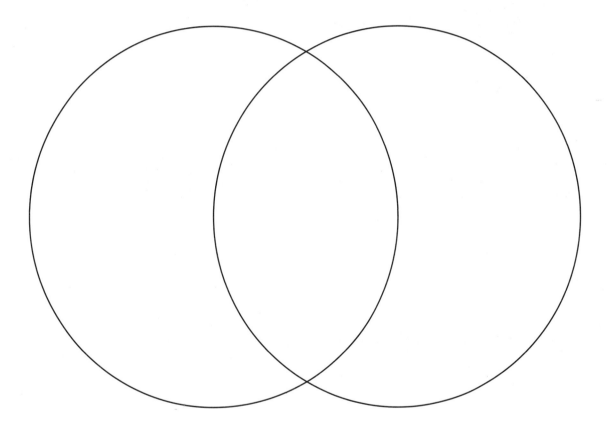

Return to the Essential Question

How do authors use different ways of telling a story?

In a small group or as a class, discuss the Essential Question. Think about what you have learned about word meanings; about the features of prose, drama, and poetry; and about telling stories from different points of view. Use evidence from the four unit texts to answer the question.

Figurative Language

Guided Instruction Authors use **figurative language** to compare things that might not seem alike. The comparisons make their writing more interesting and vivid. Here are two common types of figurative language:

- **Simile:** when the author says that one thing is *like* or *as* another

- **Metaphor:** when the author says that one thing *is* another

Look at these examples from "Bringing Hope to the Valley":

Simile	The men were like an army of skeletons...
Metaphor	...the deep snow was a blanket over the road

The simile uses the word *like* to compare the soldiers to skeletons. The comparison helps you understand the soldiers' hardships. The metaphor says that the snow *was* a blanket. The comparison helps you imagine how the snow covered everything.

Guided Practice Read this example of figurative language about James Armistead.

After the Revolutionary War, Armistead had to return to a life of enslavement. That must have been a nightmare!

1. What kind of figurative language is this? _en9Le9s_

2. What two things are being compared?

dat omost evrey boysspos

Independent Practice Write a simile and a metaphor that express how you feel about one of the characters you read about in this unit.

_____

_____

Read the following review clues for a test on the American Revolution. Think about word meanings; the features of poetry, drama, and prose; and point of view. Then answer the questions on pages 125 and 126.

American Revolution Character Clues

1 **Clue 1:** The British were a weight around our necks. As soon as the Revolution began, I joined up with my militia. The battles at Saratoga were worse than I thought, but we demonstrated to the British that we knew how to fight!

2 **Clue 2:** He rode like the wind through the night, through the dark labyrinth of confusing roads. He warned his neighbors that the British were coming.

3 **Clue 3:** (*A black man is working in the fields. A white man approaches.*)

4 **LAFAYETTE:** Is this how others have repaid your service, Armistead? They now enjoy freedom—and have kept you enslaved!

5 **Clue 4:**
She could only bring a little food.
She could only bring a little medicine.
She could only bring a little clothing.
But she could bring a large amount
    of hope.

Fill in the circle of the correct answer choice.

1. Clue 4 is written as

   ○ drama.

   ○ poetry.

   ● prose.

   ○ stage directions.

2. The first two lines of Clue 3 are

   ● dialogue.

   ○ stage directions.

   ● a cast of characters.

   ○ a journal entry.

3. In Clue 2, what is the most likely meaning of *labyrinth*, a word from an ancient myth?

   ○ tunnel

   ○ treasure

   ● battlefield

   ○ maze

4. In Clue 1, what does *demonstrated to* mean?

   ○ battled

   ○ argued with

   ○ showed

   ● acted out

5. Underline the simile in Clue 2.

6. Circle the clues that could help you figure out the meaning of *militia* in Clue 1.

7. Was the narrator of Clue 1 part of the battles at Saratoga? How do you know?

   in clue 1 it was hard

8. In Clue 3, how do you learn about Lafayette's feelings?

   it was hard

9. Rewrite Clue 2 so that it has a first-person point of view.

   it was hard

10. Find the metaphor in Clue 1. What two things does the writer compare? What does the metaphor help you to understand?

    it was hard

Introducing UNIT 6

While you read, whether it is fiction or nonfiction, you will form opinions about the events and people described based on the evidence in the text.

In Unit 5, you learned about brave and bold personalities in America's past, including Martha Washington. Did you form an opinion about the role she played in the Revolutionary War based on what you read? What pieces of evidence in the selection helped you form your opinion?

When you write an evidence-based essay, be sure to include specific details about the events and people described. Draw evidence from the text to support your position.

An effective evidence-based text is well organized. The writing should include precise words for accuracy and interest, and it should be grammatically correct.

Progress Check *Can I?*

Before Unit 6 / **After Unit 6**

☐ ☐ Draw evidence from a text to describe its setting, events, and characters.

☐ ☐ Analyze characters and events using details from a text.

☐ ☐ Provide a conclusion.

☐ ☐ Write using commas and quotation marks to mark direct speech from a text.

☐ ☐ Write using correct relative pronouns.

☐ ☐ Write using correct relative adverbs.

☐ ☐ Write using correct end punctuation for effect.

HOME◆CONNECT...

I n this unit, children will learn how to write an **evidence-based essay**. They include information (evidence) from other texts to support their writing topic idea. This helps them sharpen their skill at analyzing an event or person.

As your child reads different texts, have him or her identify the **text evidence** on which the writing is based. Do writers **describe characters, events or the setting** to support their analysis? Do writers **draw on specific details**? Discuss whether the evidence makes the writing believable or helps to shape your child's opinion on the subject.

You can do this with all kinds of writing, from opinion pieces, to biographies, to accounts of events, to blogs. Talk about the type of evidence presented and whether one kind is more persuasive than another. Explain to your child why one form of evidence might be more reliable than another.

Conversation Starter: Select a story from the week's news, whether from the newspaper, on local television, or on the Internet. Read or view the story together with your child, then highlight or write the evidence presented in the story. Look for direct quotations and specific details about people involved in the news events. Discuss with your child whether the evidence presented supports the author's or reporter's conclusion.

IN THIS UNIT, YOUR CHILD WILL...

- Learn to draw evidence from other texts to support an essay topic.

- Learn to describe characters, settings, and events in a text by drawing on specific details.

- Learn specific language skills and use them in writing an evidence-based essay.

    - Use commas and quotation marks to indicate direct speech and quotations from another text.

    - Correctly use the relative pronouns *who, whose, whom, which,* and *that* correctly.

    - Correctly use the relative adverbs *where, when,* and *why.*

    - Correctly use ending punctuation for effect.

WAYS TO HELP YOUR CHILD

As your child reads texts, ask what evidence the author presents to support his or her opinion. Discuss why the evidence is or is not convincing. Listen to your child's opinion and ask questions about what he or she thinks about the issue being discussed.

(**ONLINE**)

For more Home Connect activities, continue online at sadlierconnect.com

Research to Build and Present Knowledge: Write Evidence-Based Essays

George Washington's Headquarters at Valley Forge during the Revolutionary War

Essential Question:
How can I include evidence from other texts to support my writing?

Write Evidence-Based Essays 130

Language: Commas and Quotation Marks in Direct Quotations 134

Language: Relative Pronouns. 135

Language: Relative Adverbs 136

Language: Punctuation for Effect 137

Speaking and Listening. 138

Unit 6 Review 139

WRITE EVIDENCE-BASED ESSAYS

CREATING AN ORGANIZATIONAL STRUCTURE

Eddie has used an outline to organize his essay. It lists the specific details from the original text that support a position.

Title: _____

I. **Introduction**
   a. Topic – Identify character or events, and state view
_____
_____
_____

II. **Body**
   a. Describe character/events in original text
_____
_____

   b. Direct quotations to support your position
_____
_____

   c. Specific details that support your position
_____
_____

III. **Conclusion**
   a. Restate, wrap up view of character/events
_____
_____

INTRODUCTION

- Introduces the topic
- States a claim

DESCRIBE SETTING

To support your analysis, describe the setting of the original text using details.

Underline the details that set the scene of the original text.

Read a Student Model

Eddie just finished reading "Bringing Hope to the Valley" in Unit 5. Now he has to write a report on the role our first First Lady, Martha Washington, played in supporting the troops. He must use evidence from the original text to support his analysis. As you read Eddie's essay, think about the kind of evidence he uses.

Martha Washington Puts the Troops First

Everyone knows that George Washington is one of the founding fathers of our country. But not as many know that his wife, Martha Washington, is one of its founding mothers. She was a good leader and organizer. With her help, the Continental Army survived a terrible winter.

During the winter of 1777, General George Washington and the Continental Army were camped at Valley Forge, Pennsylvania. There was little food and clothing. The men were packed into tiny cabins that lacked heat. Many died of starvation, disease, and exposure to the elements.

Soldiers wrote to Mrs. Washington to ask for help. One soldier pleaded, "Please do what you can, ma'am. If you cannot bring us food, clothes, or medicine, at least please bring us some hope." Mrs. Washington knew she had to help the men serving in the army.

Mrs. Washington, her niece Polly, and their servants loaded carriages with all the food, clothing, cloth, and medicine that they could find at Mount Vernon. Once everything was packed, they headed to Pennsylvania.

It was a hard journey. The snow was so high that Mrs. Washington's carriages could not get through. Instead of turning back or giving up, she hired a sleigh.

Once she was in camp, Mrs. Washington worked very hard to get everything organized. Mrs. Washington gave orders like a general leading troops into battle. "Unload the sleigh! Take the food and medicine to the central camp offices. Bring the cloth to me," she ordered.

The women of the camp spent their days sewing and knitting new clothes for the soldiers. They also tended to the ill and injured soldiers in the camp hospitals. Even when the women were tired, cold, and hungry, Mrs. Washington reminded them that they couldn't stop "while so many soldiers were still cold."

DESCRIBE CHARACTERS

To support your analysis, describe characters in the original text, using their thoughts, words, or actions.

Circle Mrs. Washington's thoughts about the troops' situation.

DESCRIBE EVENTS

Describe events in the original text that support your analysis of Martha Washington.

Underline events that help show the character of Martha Washington.

USE TEXT EVIDENCE

Use quotations to support points.

Box quoted words that support Eddie's view of Martha Washington.

Mrs. Washington knew that in addition to taking care of the ill soldiers, she needed to improve the morale of the men. She and the women in the camp held parties and put on a play to help take the soldiers' minds off their situation.

Once the winter was over, life in the camp improved. Mrs. Washington's cheerful mood spread throughout the camp. The soldiers had warm clothes and food. They were well enough to once again practice military drills, with Baron von Steuben leading the way.

Without Mrs. Washington's determination and leadership, the Continental Army might not have survived the winter. Her efforts made certain that the soldiers were able to continue the fight for our new nation.

CONCLUSION

Eddie uses the evidence presented earlier to wrap up his analysis of Martha Washington and the camp.

Circle Eddie's summary of how Martha Washington helped save the soldiers' lives.

Use an outline like the one below to organize your evidence-based essay on a character or an event you've read about. Be sure to describe characters, setting, and events, and use quotations and specific details to support your points. Then write a first draft of your essay on a separate piece of paper. You will use this draft to write your final essay in the Unit 6 Review section on page 140.

Title: _____

I. **Introduction**

    a. Topic – Identify character or events, and state view

    _____

    _____

    _____

II. **Body**

    a. Describe character/events in original text

    _____

    _____

    b. Direct quotations to support your position

    _____

    _____

    c. Specific details that support your position

    _____

    _____

III. **Conclusion**

    a. Restate, wrap up view of character/events

    _____

    _____

Commas and Quotation Marks in Direct Quotations

Guided Instruction Writers use **commas and quotation marks** to set dialogue or speech apart from the rest of the text. These marks help readers identify the person speaking.

- *"I don't want to go home," the four-year-old cried.*

- *The baker said, "We only have two loaves of bread left."*

- *Clarissa raised her hand and asked, "Can you repeat the question?"*

- *The novel* Charlotte's Web *begins, "Where's Papa going with that ax?"*

Guided Practice Add commas and quotation marks where they are needed in these sentences.

1. Please put your shoes away   said Mom.

2. The play will begin in 15 minutes   announced the usher.

3. As they left for the park, Marissa complained   It's too hot to go outside.

4. General Douglas MacArthur is known for the words   I shall return.

5. That answer is correct   replied the teacher.

Independent Practice Write four sentences that include dialogue. Be sure to use commas and quotation marks.

1. _____

_____

2. _____

_____

3. _____

_____

4. _____

_____

Relative Pronouns

Guided Instruction A relative clause is a part of a sentence that has a subject and verb and modifies a noun. A relative clause begins with a relative pronoun: *who, whose, whom, which,* and *that.* **Relative pronouns** refer to the noun that comes before them in the sentence. Example: *This is the house **that Jack built**.* The relative pronoun *that* refers to the noun *house.*

Kind of Noun	Relative Pronoun	Example Sentences
a person	*who, whose, whom, that*	*Beth, who takes gymnastics, is flexible.* *Lily, whose hair is curly, wore a hat.* *The person whom I talked to has left.* *He was a man that spoke few words.*
a thing	*which, that, whose*	*The sofa, which was new, was Jane's favorite place to nap.* *This is the cake that Henry baked.* *The book, whose author lives in town, became a bestseller.*

Guided Practice In each sentence, underline the relative pronoun twice and the noun it refers to once.

1. I petted the dog that wagged its tail.

2. My brother, whose picture is in the paper, won the race on Saturday.

3. The alarm, which was very loud, would not stop ringing.

Independent Practice Write the correct relative pronoun in each sentence.

1. I have a friend _____ dog is afraid of thunder.

2. The fruit _____ was on the counter needs to be put in the refrigerator.

3. The person _____ sent me the package is my best friend.

Relative Adverbs

Guided Instruction **Relative adverbs** are the words that tell you the where, when, or why of a sentence. They introduce an adverb clause. A clause is a group of related words with a subject and a verb that is part of a sentence.

- *The house **where he lives** is the blue one.*

- *The day **when I adopted my puppy** was the best.*

- *There must be some reason **why the child cried**.*

Guided Practice Underline the relative adverb in each sentence below.

1. The store where I bought my new jacket is closing.

2. I look forward to Monday, when a brand new week begins.

3. The feeling of freedom is the reason why I love running.

Write the correct relative adverb in each sentence.

1. June and July are the months _____ the pool is open.

2. This is the hospital _____ my mother works.

3. Watching the scary movie was the reason _____ I slept with the lights on.

Independent Practice Write three sentences of your own using the relative adverbs *where, when,* and *why*.

1. _____

_____

2. _____

_____

3. _____

_____

Punctuation for Effect

Guided Instruction There are four types of sentences in English and three **ending punctuation marks**. The way in which you punctuate a sentence helps a reader understand what effect you are trying to achieve. The same words in a sentence with different punctuation can have different meanings.

- The **declarative** makes a statement and ends with a period (.).

  I will watch that dog.

- The **interrogative** asks a question and ends with a question mark (?).

  Will you watch that dog?

- The **exclamatory** expresses emotion like anger, excitement, or surprise and ends with an exclamation point (!).

  Watch that dog!

- The **imperative** gives a command and ends with a period or an exclamation mark.

  Watch that dog.

Guided Practice Read each sentence and write which sentence type it is, based on its ending punctuation mark.

1. I got an A on my project! _____

2. Who left this mess in the kitchen? _____

3. I need you to sit down now! _____

4. On rainy days, I love to stay in bed and read. _____

Independent Practice Write three different types of sentences using a different ending punctuation mark in each sentence.

1. _____

2. _____

3. _____

Discuss the Essential Question

How can I include evidence from other texts to support my writing?

Think about the Essential Question by responding to the questions below. Support your position with evidence from the text.

1. What evidence from the original text did the writer use to support his analysis of Martha Washington?

_____

_____

2. What specific details did the writer include to describe the setting of the events?

_____

_____

Use your notes above to discuss the Essential Question in small groups or as a class. Follow agreed-upon rules for discussion. Use the organizer below to record what you heard and how you participated.

	Ideas I Agree or Disagree With	Questions I Asked
Agree		
Disagree		
	New Ideas I Had During Discussion	**Questions I Answered**

This paragraph has incorrect relative pronouns and relative adverbs. It also has a missing comma and quotation marks to set off dialogue, and incorrect ending punctuation. Write the paragraph correctly on the lines below.

In December 1777, General George Washington and his troops made an encampment at Valley Forge, Pennsylvania. The soldiers were hungry and tired where they arrived. Conditions were so bad that General Washington wrote this army must inevitably. . . starve, dissolve or disperse. Despite the hardships, after six months the soldiers whose survived emerged as a unified fighting force. They went on to successfully beat the British army at the Battle of Monmouth? After reading about the terrible winter, do you think you would have stayed with the Continental Army.

_____

_____

_____

_____

_____

_____

_____

_____

_____

_____

Assignment: Write an evidence-based essay on a character or event you've read about.

On the lines below, write your final copy of the evidence-based essay you created on page 133. Be sure to use specific evidence from the original text and descriptions of characters, events, or setting to support your position. Conclude your essay with a restatement of your position. See the Writing Handbook (pages 275–283) for ways to improve your writing as you revise.

_____

_____

_____

_____

_____

_____

_____

_____

_____

_____

_____

_____

_____

_____

_____

_____

_____

_____

There are three parts to this performance task. Your teacher will provide you with copies of three selections.

- *Setting Coral Free* Genre: Realistic Fiction
- *Rachel Carson* Genre: Biography
- *Underwater Cities Under Threat* Genre: Informational Text

Part 1: Literary Analysis

☐ Read *Setting Coral Free* carefully. Take notes that will help you understand the passage.

☐ Answer Items 1–3 on pages 142–143.

☐ Then read the prompt for Item 4 and write two paragraphs on your own paper. You may w`ant to make some notes on scratch paper first.

Part 2: Narrative Writing

☐ Read *Rachel Carson* carefully. Take notes that will help you understand the passage.

☐ Answer Items 1–2 on page 144.

☐ Then read the prompt for Item 3 and write two or three paragraphs on your own paper. You may want to make some notes on scratch paper first.

Part 3: Research Simulation

☐ Read *Underwater Cities Under Threat* carefully. Take notes that will help you understand the passage.

☐ Answer Items 1–3 about *Underwater Cities Under Threat* on pages 145–146.

☐ Review *Rachel Carson*. You will use it in addition to *Underwater Cities Under Threat* in this task.

☐ Then read the prompt for Item 4 and write an essay on your own paper. You may want to make some notes on scratch paper first.

Part 1 Literary Analysis

Read all parts of the question before responding. Circle the correct answer to Items 1–3. Use your own paper to respond to Item 4.

Item 1

Part A In *Setting Coral Free*, why did Martin raise his hand in class?

a. He likes to take part in the discussions led by Ms. Price.

b. He wanted to tell about the sea turtle he held.

c. Ms. Price asks him a question about marine life.

d. Janet was concerned about the sea turtle.

Part B Which sentence from the story supports the answer to Part A?

a. "He surprised himself because he didn't usually volunteer to speak."

b. "She showed the class several photographs of ocean animals."

c. "Janet smiled, and several other students asked questions."

d. "Martin was proud that he had information to share."

Item 2

Part A In the story *Setting Coral Free*, why does Martin feel sad when it is time to release Coral?

a. Coral is no longer a baby sea turtle.

b. Several sea turtles at the hospital are hurt.

c. He feels a connection to Coral because he named her, and will miss her.

d. Martin could not ride next to his grandpa in the boat.

Part B Which detail from the story best supports the answer to Part A?

a. "Most of them were injured, but Martin knew they were in good hands."

b. "When it was time to release Coral, Martin patted the top of her head."

c. "Martin was surprised to see that Coral had grown so much."

d. "Martin sat at the back of the boat with the hospital staff."

Item 3

Part A What does the word *funds* mean in this line from *Setting Coral Free*?

They spent weeks raising *funds* to help the sea turtle.

a. information

b. ideas

c. programs

d. money

Part B Which sentence from the story best helps the reader understand the meaning of *funds*?

a. "We can ask people for money that will help the hospital."

b. "Ms. Price and all his classmates were excited by the idea."

c. "When they filled out the adoption forms, Ms. Price asked."

d. "The hospital has an adoption program."

Item 4

Think about why Martin's experience with Coral was important. How did his experience make a difference? How would the ending be different if Martin had not known Coral? Write two paragraphs to explain your answer. Use details from the story to help your answer.

Part 2 Narrative Writing

Read all parts of the question before responding. Circle the correct answer to Items 1–2. Use your own paper to respond to Item 3.

Item 1

Part A   What is the main idea of *Rachel Carson*?

   a. Carson was the author of the book *The Sea Around Us*.

   b. Carson loved the ocean and wanted to write about it.

   c. Carson was a determined author who kept trying for success.

   d. Carson's books affected people's understanding of marine ecology.

Part B   Which sentence from the text best supports the answer to Part A?

   a. "Her fascination with the ocean grew as she learned more."

   b. "Carson changed how people thought about the environment."

   c. "Carson's second book was titled *The Sea Around Us*."

   d. "She wanted to spend her time writing and enjoying her beloved ocean."

Item 2

Part A   What is the meaning of ***fascination*** in this sentence from the text?

Her ***fascination*** with the ocean grew as she learned more.

   a. visits   **b.** interest   **c.** decisions   **d.** protection

Part B   Which detail from the text helps the reader understand the meaning of ***fascination***?

   a. Carson made ecology popular in her books.

   b. Carson loved the ocean long before she saw it.

   c. Carson was an adult when she finally saw the ocean.

   d. Carson wrote a second book after the first one didn't do well.

Item 3

Think about the events described in *Rachel Carson*. What happened after Rachel Carson published *The Sea Around Us*? Write two or three paragraphs describing what you think might have happened to Rachel Carson next. Use ideas and facts from the text to help your writing.

Part 3 Research Simulation

Read all parts of the question before responding. Circle the correct answer to Items 1–3. Use your own paper to respond to Item 4.

Item 1

Part A In *Underwater Cities Under Threat*, why are coral reefs important?

- **a.** They come in different shapes.
- **b.** They are shaped by water currents.
- **c.** They provide a home for other animals.
- **d.** They are food for all the animals that live there.

Part B Which sentence from the text supports the answer to Part A?

- **a.** "Their shape depends on the type of coral polyps that make them."
- **b.** "The coral reefs give them protection from their predators"
- **c.** "The coral protects the land by breaking up the waves"
- **d.** "Coral reefs in some parts of the world are dying off."

Item 2

Part A What is the main idea of *Underwater Cities Under Threat*?

- **a.** Coral reefs are an important source of income for people.
- **b.** Coral reefs are delicate ecosystems that must be protected.
- **c.** Coral reefs are damaged by climate change and pollution.
- **d.** Coral reefs are formed by coral polyps that live in colonies.

Part B Which sentence from the text best supports the answer to Part A?

- **a.** "They spend money while visiting the reefs"
- **b.** "These structures grow inch by inch to form coral reefs."
- **c.** "Coral reefs are found in warm waters that are clear and shallow."
- **d.** "But coral reefs are at risk of dying out unless people take action."

Item 3

Part A   Which dictionary entry below best defines *colonies* as it is used in this sentence from the text?

"Coral polyps live in *colonies*."

col·o·ny ('kä-lə-nē) *plural* colonies

1. an area under the control of a more powerful country

2. one of the 13 areas of land that later became the United States

3. a group of plants or animals of one type that live and grow near each other

4. a group of people who are alike in some way and live together in a place

    a. 1   **b.** 2   **c.** 3   **d.** 4

Part B   Which key words in the Part A dictionary entries help the reader know which entry is the correct definition?

a. in a place

b. who are alike

c. areas of land

d. plants or animals

Item 4

You have read two texts about marine ecology. Think about the facts in *Rachel Carson* and *Underwater Cities Under Threat*. Why are marine ecosystems important to people? What are the different ways someone can help protect marine ecosystems? Write two or three paragraphs to explain your answer. Use details from both passages to support your answer.

Introducing UNIT 7

Have you ever solved a tough problem or challenge? How did your solution make things better? In this unit, you will read about challenges that people faced, both long ago and today. In each case, they solved these problems and made their world a better place.

This unit focuses on social studies and science topics. It includes a historical text, an explanatory text, a biography, and a personal essay. These are called informational texts, for each one shares facts about a topic. Authors who write informational texts organize their writing clearly. Within the structure of their writing, they present interesting details. Sometimes they also include unfamiliar words that you can figure out by using clues in the text.

You can learn a lot from reading an informational text and from comparing texts about the same topic. Let's see what you can learn as you read these next few texts!

Progress Check *Can I?*

Before Unit 7

After Unit 7

☐ Determine the meaning of academic and content-area words. ☐

☐ Describe the overall structure of an informational text. ☐

☐ Compare and contrast two accounts of the same event. ☐

☐ Use synonyms and antonyms to check the meanings of words. ☐

HOME◆CONNECT...

IN THIS UNIT, YOUR CHILD WILL...

- Use clues in a text to figure out the meanings of unfamiliar words or words with multiple meanings.

- Describe text structure—how information and ideas are related—in an informational text.

- Identify problems and solutions or causes and effects discussed in a text.

- Compare and contrast a firsthand account and a secondhand account of the same event.

- Show an understanding of words by relating them to words with similar meanings (synonyms) or opposite meanings (antonyms).

- Compare and contrast four texts on the same theme: an historical text, an explanatory text, and two memoirs paired with biographies.

WAYS TO HELP YOUR CHILD

Discuss the facts relating to a recent news event, listing any questions your child might have about the event. Brainstorm various ways to search for answers, such as on the Internet or in a newspaper. Work with your child to answer one or two questions on the list. Then talk about what you learned.

Writers of informational text often include clues that help readers **determine the meaning of unfamiliar words**. Choose a print or online article about a topic that your child might enjoy. Highlight any unfamiliar words. Then invite your child to work with you to find clues that help you figure out their meanings.

The structure of a text is critical for making informational text clear. Problem and solution is one type of text structure. Writers explain a problem or challenge and the solution that helped fix it. Talk with your child about a problem your family, friends, or community once faced. Discuss how this problem was solved. Then work together to write a short (half-page) article about it to share with the family.

Comparing and contrasting firsthand and secondhand accounts can help readers gain a deeper understanding of an event and the people involved in it. With your child, watch a TV news program that includes an interview with a person who experienced an event firsthand. Compare and contrast the reporter's account of the event with the interview account.

Conversation Starter: Share with your child a time from your childhood when you solved a problem or did something to make a situation better. Challenge your child to tell a story about what he or she would have done in your place. Then talk about the similarities and differences in your stories. Explain that even though the two of you described the same story situation, you talked about it in different ways.

ONLINE

For more Home Connect activities, continue online at sadlierconnect.com

Reading Informational Text: Craft and Structure

Essential Question:
How can authors support their purpose in writing an informational text?

Determining Word
Meanings 150

Describing Text
Structures 156

Comparing and Contrasting
Events and Topics 162

Close Reading 168

Connect Across Texts 173

Language:
Synonyms and Antonyms . . .174

Unit 7 Review 175

DETERMINING WORD MEANINGS

WORDS TO KNOW

confederacy

diverse

strife

To **determine the meaning of an unfamiliar word**, you can consult a **dictionary** or use **context clues** from the sentence or nearby sentences.

CITE EVIDENCE

A **Synonyms** are words with the same or similar meanings, such as *enormous* and *huge*. Sometimes, synonyms can help make the meanings of unfamiliar words clear. In paragraph 3, circle *woodlands* and its synonym.

B Using clues from the text, you often can **infer**, or figure out, the meaning of an unfamiliar word. In paragraph 3, underline a clue that helps you understand *permanent*. What do you think the word means?

The People of the Longhouse

(Genre: Historical Text)

1   New York State has a **diverse** population because different kinds of people live and work there. This is true today and it was true in the past. Centuries ago, the place we now call New York was home to diverse nations of American Indians. They lived in different territories and had different governments, but six of these groups found a way to live in peace. Together, they formed the Iroquois Confederacy.

2   A **confederacy** is a group of people or nations that support and protect one another. The Iroquois Confederacy included five American Indian nations: the Mohawk, the Oneida, the Onondaga, the Cayuga, and the Seneca. They came together sometime before the early 1600s. A sixth nation, the Tuscarora, joined in the early 1700s.

3   The Iroquois nations lived in the woodlands located south of Lake Ontario and east of the Finger Lakes. These forests provided the people with everything they needed to survive. The people used trees to construct homes for permanent villages that they lived in all year long. They hunted deer and other forest animals for food and resources. They also created clearings to plant corn, beans, and squash. These crops were known as the "Three Sisters."

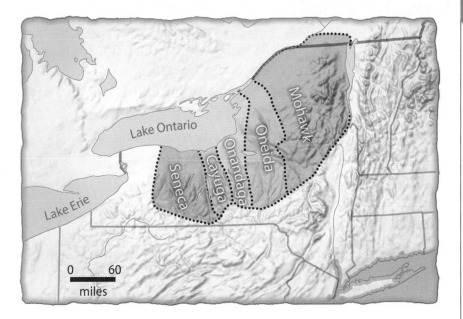

CITE EVIDENCE

C Sometimes, the text **restates** what a word means, similar to a definition. Circle the word *retaliated* in paragraph 4 and underline the words that restate its meaning.

D **Antonyms** are words that are opposite in meaning, like *inside* and *outside*. Sometimes, antonyms can be used as context clues. In paragraph 5, put a box around the word *peace* and its antonym. How are the two words different?

4   Before the Iroquois Confederacy formed, the American Indian groups of the region often fought. War parties from the different nations raided each other. There were even attacks within nations. If one person killed another, the victim's family members often retaliated, or struck back in revenge. People lived in fear, and many wondered if it would ever be possible to feel safe and secure.

5   A Huron man named Dekanawidah (duh-kah-nah-WEE-duh) thought that things could be better. He believed that different nations could live in peace, so he left the Huron nation and traveled into Mohawk territory. Everywhere he went, he talked to people about the need to end the fighting. He called his message "The Great Peace." Dekanawidah met an Onondaga man named Hiawatha (high-uh-WAH-thuh). They decided to meet with leaders from the other nations to bring an end to the **strife**.

Comprehension Check

How does learning the meaning of *confederacy* in the text help you understand the importance of this time in early American history?

The People of the Longhouse *continued*

WORDS TO KNOW

colonist

democracy

longhouse

sachem

CITE EVIDENCE

A Underline two clues in paragraph 7 that help you understand what the word *constitution* means.

B Read paragraph 8. Circle a clue that can help you understand what *council* means. Discuss your ideas with a partner and then check the definition in a dictionary. Were your meanings close?

6   Dekanawidah and Hiawatha explained that the nations of this region had much in common. They spoke similar languages, had similar cultures, and all made their homes in the area's forests. The two men persuaded the five nations to form a league because they were better off uniting than fighting. For his efforts, Dekanawidah became known as "the Great Peacemaker." (However, his own people, the Hurons, chose not to join the confederacy.)

7   After forming the confederacy, the five nations agreed on a set of rules that became known as the Iroquois Constitution. A constitution is a plan of government. Because the Iroquois Confederacy was a **democracy**, everyone had the power to say how things were done. No single nation had authority over the others.

8   The nations formed a council that solved problems to avoid warfare. Council members, called **sachems**, represented the interests of each nation. Only men served on the council. However, women played an important role, for they had the power to select or remove council members. The council recorded their treaties or laws on belts with detailed patterns of beads, known as wampum.

9   Together, the five nations called themselves the Haudenosaunee (hoo-dee-noh-SHAW-nee) people. European **colonists** who later came to the region called them the Iroquois. Today, these groups may be called either name.

10   The word *Haudenosaunee* means "people of the longhouse." Many Iroquois lived in homes called **longhouses**. A longhouse was just what you might think: a very long house. Up to fifty people lived in each one. The residents were all part of an extended family. If the family grew bigger, the house could be made longer.

Comprehension Check

1. In paragraph 7, which synonym helps you figure out the meaning of the word *authority*?

  a. confederacy

  b. power

  c. nation

  d. constitution

2. From clues in paragraph 10, you can figure out that *residents* are

  a. members of an extended family.

  b. members of a particular nation.

  c. people living in a certain place.

  d. builders of places to live.

3. Work with a partner to reread paragraph 6. Discuss what you think the word *league* means. What clues in the text did you use to determine the meaning? Then use a print or online dictionary to look up the word. Did you figure out the correct meaning?

It mean to live some where

DETERMINING WORD MEANINGS

The People of the Longhouse *continued*

WORDS TO KNOW

lacrosse

symbolic

CITE EVIDENCE

A In paragraph 14, put a box around a phrase that is a synonym for the word *colonists*. Think about how synonyms and antonyms can help you understand the meaning of unfamiliar words.

B Circle the word *immunity* in paragraph 14. Identify text that restates the meaning of this word. Underline it.

11   A longhouse was constructed from tree bark and wooden poles. There was a doorway at each end, covered with animal skins to keep out the cold and rain. Openings in the roof let out smoke from cooking fires. Inside, platforms built along the sides were used for sleeping and storage.

12   The Haudenosaunee saw their confederacy as a **symbolic** longhouse that stretched across their combined territories. The Mohawk nation was in the east, at the "eastern door." The Seneca nation was in the west, at the "western door."

13   The Haudenosaunee also were known for playing a ball game we now call **lacrosse**. Two teams of players used long sticks with nets attached at the ends to catch or toss a ball. The game taught young people how to work together as a team. Today, many Iroquois continue to enjoy playing lacrosse.

14   In the 1600s and 1700s, European colonists came into contact with the area's native people. The Iroquois traded with the settlers and acquired new tools. However, the Iroquois suffered in a number of ways. They were exposed to new diseases, such as smallpox. They did not have immunity to these diseases, which means their bodies could not fight them off. Many Iroquois died as a result. They also battled with the newcomers, losing many lives.

15   Not all contact between the colonists and the Haudenosaunee led to problems, though. As the American colonies became free from British rule, leaders of the new nation began to create a government. They looked to the Haudenosaunee as an example, and the Iroquois Constitution became a model for the United States Constitution.

16   Hundreds of years after the creation of the Iroquois Confederacy, many Haudenosaunee continue to live in New York State. The confederacy still exists, and leaders from the six nations make up the council. The "Great Peace" remains an important part of their way of life. This idea showed that it was possible to make the world a better place.

Comprehension Check

(MORE ONLINE) **sadlierconnect.com**

1. Which of the following is the best meaning of the word *platform*? Look for text clues in paragraph 11.

   a. a type of bed

   b. a beam or support

   c. a small, round opening

   d. a raised, flat surface

2. In paragraph 15, what is a synonym clue for the word *model*?

   a. constitution

   b. example

   c. government

   d. rule

3. How does the text information about longhouses help you understand why the longhouse was called *symbolic* of the Iroquois Confederacy?

It was called that because symbolic longhouse that stretched across their combined territories.

WORDS TO KNOW

inspection

reservoir

sandhog

valve

Text structure is the way a text is organized. Different texts have different structures.

CITE EVIDENCE

A **Problem/solution** is one type of text structure. In this text, paragraph 1 states a problem: The water around New York City is too salty or too dirty to use. Put a box around the sentence in that paragraph that introduces the solution.

B Look ahead to paragraph 4. Underline the sentences in that paragraph that name new problems. Why are these major problems for New Yorkers?

A Tale of a City's Tunnels
(Genre: Explanatory Text)

1   Millions of people reside in New York City. Every day, they use billions of gallons of water—for drinking, cooking, bathing, washing, and even flushing. New Yorkers cannot depend on water from the area's rivers, which is either too salty or too dirty to use. So, how do the people get the water they need? They rely on a system of tunnels that delivers fresh water each day.

2   The first water tunnel opened in 1917. The second was completed in 1935. Both transport water into New York City from the Hillview Reservoir. A **reservoir** is a man-made lake, created to collect water. The Hillview Reservoir is in Yonkers, just north of the city. It supplies about 90 percent of New York City's water.

3   Tunnel Number 1 is about 18 miles long. It runs from the Hillview Reservoir through the Bronx, into Manhattan, and then into Brooklyn. Tunnel Number 2 runs from the reservoir through the Bronx and into Queens and Brooklyn. It is 20 miles long. When it was completed, it was the longest water tunnel in the world.

CITE EVIDENCE

C In paragraph 5, what is the solution to the problems discussed in paragraph 4? Put a box around the sentence that identifies this solution.

D Identify a problem discussed in paragraph 6. Circle the text that explains the problem and the details that are solutions to it. Do you think the solutions sound helpful? Why or why not?

4   However, those two tunnels have not been enough. As the city's population has grown, New York has needed more and more water. That is not the only problem. Today, both tunnels need work. They have serious leaks, and the **valves** that control the flow of water are old. If these problems get worse, the tunnels could collapse. That would be a disaster! However, the tunnels cannot be shut down for **inspection** and repair because the city depends on them.

5   As a result, New York City decided to build a third water tunnel. Construction began in 1970 and will finish in 2018. The Department of Environmental Protection (DEP) oversees the job.

6   Workers called **sandhogs** dig and construct the new tunnel. Many of their ancestors worked on older water tunnels and on tunnels for cars, sewers, and subways in the city. Because this kind of work can be difficult and dangerous, sandhogs must wear hardhats. They also have to follow many safety precautions.

Comprehension Check

What problem did New York City begin to solve in 1970? How will this solution help the city? Cite text evidence.

DESCRIBING TEXT STRUCTURES

Guided Practice

A Tale of a City's Tunnels *continued*

WORDS TO KNOW

bedrock

distribution

site

technology

CITE EVIDENCE

A What problem is discussed in paragraph 8? Underline the text that explains it.

B Think about the problem discussed in paragraph 9. Circle the text that identifies it. How would you solve that problem?

The TBM is a huge tunnel-boring machine.

7   Water Tunnel Number 3 is one of the most complex construction projects in the world. It is also the biggest building job in New York City's history. The completed tunnel will run from the Hillview Reservoir through the Bronx and Manhattan, then into Queens and Brooklyn.

8   City planners needed to find a way to tackle such a difficult job. Constructing the tunnel in stages seemed to be the best solution. The first part of the tunnel was finished in 1998, and it greatly improved the city's **distribution** of drinking water. The second section of the tunnel was finished in 2013. The third and fourth sections will be done by 2018.

9   The DEP is building the tunnel deep below the city in **bedrock**. This type of rock is very solid and not easy to drill through. So in 2003, the agency decided to try a tunnel-boring machine (TBM). The TBM has 27 steel cutters that rotate to drill a hole through bedrock. This type of **technology** had never been used in the city before. It helped solve several problems. The equipment works twice as fast as the old drill-and-blast method. It also does not make too much noise, which pleases people above the construction **sites**!

10   The tunnel-boring machine is about 70 feet long, which could have
been a problem. It would have been very difficult to lower such a
massive machine 600 feet below ground. However, the TBM was put
together in such a way that it could be sent to the construction sites in
pieces and assembled there.

Comprehension Check

1. What is the solution to the problem discussed in paragraph 8?

   a. The tunnel is being built in stages.

   b. The path of the tunnel has been changed.

   c. The tunnel has improved water distribution.

   d. The workers take safety precautions.

2. What is the solution to the problem discussed in paragraph 9?

   a. The construction site has been located 600 feet below ground.

   b. The tunnel is being built through bedrock.

   c. The TBM can be taken apart and put back together.

   d. The DEP has decided to use a tunnel-boring machine.

3. How does the information about the TBM fit the problem/solution
structure of this text? Use details from the text in your answer.

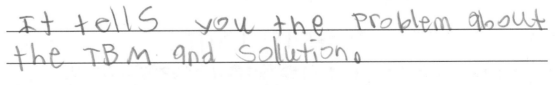

_It tells you the problem about
the TBM and solution._

DESCRIBING TEXT STRUCTURES

Independent Practice

WORDS TO KNOW

chamber

disruption

supply shaft

CITE EVIDENCE

A Identify a solution discussed in paragraph 11. Underline the text that explains why this solution is helpful.

B Underline the problem discussed in paragraph 13. What solution is mentioned in the text? What do you think of that solution?

11   The tunnel-boring machine was not the only big solution the DEP has found. The agency also placed water valves in separate **chambers**. Separating them will make them much easier to maintain and repair in the future.

12   One other problem needed to be solved. Tunnel Number 3 is deep underground. The DEP had to find a way to deliver water from this depth to the people of the city. So, they have begun to build **supply shafts**, which will send water to the surface. Each supply shaft is a tube that is 20 feet wide and runs 60 stories down.

13   So far, this work has posed some problems. Tunnel digging happens far below the surface, so it does not disturb the people who live above. However, workers drill supply shafts from street level. This work makes a lot of noise and causes **disruptions**. People in these communities have had to learn to live with the construction around them.

14   It will all be worth it in the end, though. In 2006, New York City mayor Michael Bloomberg said this about Tunnel Number 3: "Future generations of New Yorkers will have the clean and reliable supply of drinking water essential for our growing city." Also, when the tunnel is finished, the city can finally drain, inspect, and repair Tunnel Number 1 and Tunnel Number 2.

Hillview Reservoir in
Yonkers, New York

15   Fixing both water tunnels will help make sure that New Yorkers have all the water they need for many years to come. Together, these three tunnels will make New York City a better place.

Statistics for Tunnel Number 3
Location: The tunnel sits 600 feet below New York City.
Length: The entire tunnel will be 60 miles long.
Equipment: Workers use a tunnel-boring machine to drill.
Materials: Workers use concrete to construct the tunnel.
Cost: The total cost of the project is $6 billion.

Comprehension Check   (MORE ONLINE) sadlierconnect.com

1. The DEP solved the problem discussed in paragraph 12 by

   a. transporting water into the city.

   b. constructing supply shafts.

   c. building the tunnel deep underground.

   d. placing water valves in chambers.

2. Which of the following best describes the problem discussed in paragraph 13?

   a. the noise made by drilling at street level

   b. the massive cost of a very long project

   c. the threat to the city's water supply

   d. the difficulty of repairing the older tunnels

3. Why is Water Tunnel Number 3 a solution for several problems in New York City? Use information from the text in your answer.

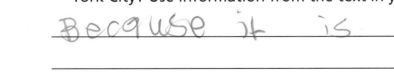
Because it is a chamber.

_____

_____

_____

WORDS TO KNOW

biography

conclusion

vexation

A description of an event is either a **firsthand account** or a **secondhand account**, depending on who is telling it.

CITE EVIDENCE

A In a **secondhand account**, the narrator is not part of the event. In paragraph 1, underline a sentence that shows that the narrator was not from Franklin's time.

B In a secondhand account, the narrator can know things that the subject does not. In paragraph 1, put a star by something that Franklin (the subject) could not know. Why do you think the narrator mentions it?

Ben Franklin's Whistle

(Genre: Memoir/Biography)

1   We often remember Benjamin Franklin (1706–1790) for his wise advice. You probably have heard some of his sayings, such as "A penny saved is a penny earned" and "Early to bed, and early to rise, makes a man healthy, wealthy, and wise." Indeed, many of Franklin's ideas were about working hard and saving money. It might not surprise him that his picture appears on the 100-dollar bill!

2   Where did Franklin learn this helpful advice? Today, we usually think of him as an older man. As a child, however, Franklin had adventures that taught him lessons about life and money.

3   Here are two stories about an experience that Franklin had as a child. Franklin tells the first story himself, in a letter. The second one comes from a **biography** about Franklin.

4   TO MADAME BRILLON.

November 10, 1779

I am charmed with your description of Paradise, and with your plan of living there; and I approve much of your **conclusion**, that, in the mean time, we should draw all the good we can from this world. In my opinion, we might all draw more good from it than we do, and suffer less evil, if we would take care not to give too much for *whistles*. . . .

5   When I was a child of seven years old, my friends, on a holiday, filled my pocket with coppers. I went directly to a shop where they sold toys for children; and being charmed with the sound of a whistle that I met by the way in the hands of another boy, I voluntarily offered and gave all my money for one. I then came home and went whistling all over the house, much pleased with my whistle, but disturbing all the family. My brothers, and sisters, and cousins, understanding the bargain I had made, told me I had given four times as much for it as it was worth; put me in mind of what good things I might have bought with the rest of the money; and laughed at me so much for my folly, that I cried with **vexation**; and the reflection gave me more chagrin than the whistle gave me pleasure.

Comprehension Check

Compare paragraphs 1–3 with paragraphs 4–5. What words are used to refer to Franklin in each? What type of information is provided in each?

CITE EVIDENCE

C A **firsthand account** of an event is told by someone who was there, usually in a first-person point of view. In the first sentence of paragraph 5, circle the pronouns that show that this narrator was part of the events.

D Firsthand accounts often include the writer's thoughts and feelings. Underline three details in paragraph 5 that show Franklin's feelings. How do these details help you understand him?

Guided Practice

Ben Franklin's Whistle *continued*

WORDS TO KNOW

charity

impression

miser

CITE EVIDENCE

A The narrator of paragraphs 1–3 mentioned Franklin's "wise sayings." Underline the "wise saying" in paragraph 6.

B Circle each kind of person on whom Franklin focuses in paragraphs 8–10. What do these people want? What do they get instead?

6   This, however, was afterward of use to me, the **impression** continuing on my mind; so that often, when I was tempted to buy some unnecessary thing, I said to myself, *Don't give too much for the whistle*; and I saved my money.

7   As I grew up, came into the world, and observed the actions of men, I thought I met with many, very many, who *gave too much for the whistle. . . .*

8   When I saw another fond of popularity, constantly employing himself in political bustles, neglecting his own affairs, and ruining them by that neglect, *He pays, indeed*, said I, *too much for his whistle.*

9   If I knew a **miser**, who gave up every kind of comfortable living, all the pleasure of doing good to others, all the esteem of his fellow-citizens, and the joys of benevolent friendship, for the sake of accumulating wealth, *Poor man*, said I, *you pay too much for your whistle.*

10   If I see one fond of appearance, or fine clothes, fine houses, fine furniture, fine equipages, all above his fortune, for which he contracts debts and ends his days in prison, *Alas!* say I, *he has paid dear, very dear, for his whistle. . . .*

11   In short, I conceive that great part of the miseries of mankind are brought upon them by the false estimates they have made of the value of things, and by their *giving too much for their whistles.*

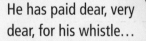

He has paid dear, very dear, for his whistle…

12   Yet I ought to have **charity** for these unhappy people, when I consider that, with all this wisdom of which I am boasting, there are certain things in the world so tempting, . . . [that] if they were put to sale, I might very easily be led to ruin myself in the purchase, and find that I had once more given too much for the *whistle*. . . .

B. Franklin
from *Memoirs of Benjamin Franklin*

Comprehension Check

1. Paragraph 6 begins by referring to "this"—the lesson that Franklin learned from the whistle experience. What was that lesson?

a. to trust no one about money matters

b. to avoid paying too much for things

c. to save his money and never spend it

d. to watch people carefully

2. How does Franklin's focus change in paragraphs 7–12?

a. He describes people who agree with him to show that he has good ideas.

b. He describes people for whom he has no sympathy.

c. He describes ways that people can waste their money.

d. He describes other ways in which people "give too much."

3. What does "paying too much for a whistle" mean to Franklin? What evidence does he use to explain this idea?

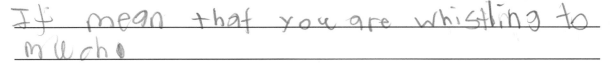

It mean that you are whistling to mucho

Independent Practice

Ben Franklin's Whistle *continued*

WORDS TO KNOW

bargain

foolish

CITE EVIDENCE

A In paragraphs 13–15, circle the words and phrases that the narrator uses to identify Benjamin Franklin.

B Underline the sentence in paragraph 20 that shows that the narrator knows something that Benjamin Franklin does not. Why is it important for you, the reader, to know this?

The Whistle
excerpt from *The Story of Benjamin Franklin*
by James Baldwin

13 Nearly two hundred years ago, there lived in Boston a little boy whose name was Benjamin Franklin.

14 On the day that he was seven years old, his mother gave him a few pennies. . . .

15 The little fellow ran out into the street. He heard the pennies jingle in his pocket as he ran. He felt as though he was very rich. . . .

16 Before Benjamin had gone very far, he met a boy blowing a whistle.

17 "That is just the thing that I want," he said. Then he hurried on to the store where all kinds of things were kept for sale.

18 "Have you any good whistles?" he asked. . . .

19 "Yes, plenty of them," said the man.

20 "Well, I want one, and I'll give you all the money I have for it," said the little fellow. He forgot to ask the price.

21 "How much money have you?" asked the man.

22 Benjamin took the coppers from his pocket. The man counted them and said, "All right, my boy. It's a **bargain**."

23 Benjamin Franklin was a proud and happy boy. He ran home as fast as he could, blowing his whistle as he ran.

24 His mother met him at the door and said, "Well, my child, what did you do with your pennies?"

25 "I bought a whistle!" he cried. "Just hear me blow it!"

26   One of his brothers was standing by and asked to see the whistle. "Well, well!" he said, "did you spend all of your money for this thing?"

27   "Every penny," said Benjamin. . . .

28   His brother laughed and said, "You are a very **foolish** fellow. You paid four times as much as it is worth."

29   The little boy saw what a mistake he had made. The whistle did not please him any more. He threw it upon the floor, and began to cry. But his mother took him upon her lap and said:

30   "Never mind, my child. We must all live and learn; and I think that my little boy will be careful, after this, not to pay too dear for his whistles."

Comprehension Check

MORE ONLINE   sadlierconnect.com

1. Which two people or groups appear in both accounts?

   a. Franklin and another boy with a whistle

   b. Franklin's mother and brother

   c. Franklin's friends and cousins

   d. Franklin and the man who made the whistle

2. Compare Franklin's letter with this account. Which of these details appears only in Franklin's letter?

   a. Franklin wants a whistle very badly.

   b. Franklin pays too much money for the whistle.

   c. Franklin thinks that some people pay too much for what they want.

   d. Franklin's mother explains a lesson for him to learn.

3. How is the focus of this story different from the focus in the letter?

The focus in the story is different because the story is a asa and a letter is not.

Helping the Union

(Genre: Cause/Effect Essay)

1   Julia Ward Howe wanted to make a difference in the world. In the 1800s, women were expected only to marry and raise children, and that is what her husband Samuel wanted. Howe loved her family, but she wanted more.

2   Howe began her career by publishing a book of poems. Readers were shocked: The poems told of her feelings and her challenges to her husband's authority. Although Samuel was not very happy that his wife was working as an author, he did not stop her. In fact, he sometimes asked her to help write and edit his newspaper.

3   Howe was also very interested in the reform movement, which was trying to make society better. She had a special concern for abolition; she wanted to see slavery come to an end in the United States. Slowly, other Northerners came to agree with that view.

4   When the Civil War began in 1861, Howe wanted to help the Union cause. At first, she thought that the idea was absurd—that in a war, only men could make a difference. However, Samuel was too old to fight, and her sons were too young. As a woman, could she help in any way?

5   Some women worked in military hospitals, but Howe could not leave her children. Instead, she found a novel way to help the Union cause. On a trip to visit soldiers, some friends sang a popular song called "John Brown's Body." Howe had wanted to write new words for the song's melody, but she had not yet been able to think of any.

6   Early the next morning, new words to the song came to her mind. Howe wrote them down, creating a song called "Battle Hymn of the Republic." Later, in her autobiography, Howe described how the song was created:

7   *I could not leave my nursery to follow the march of our armies, neither had I the practical deftness which the preparing and packing of sanitary stores demanded. Something seemed to say to me, "You would be glad to serve, but you cannot help anyone; you have nothing to give, and there is nothing for you to do." Yet, because of my sincere desire, a word was given me to say. . . .*

8   *I went to bed that night as usual, and slept, according to my wont, quite soundly. I awoke in the gray of the morning twilight; and as I lay waiting for the dawn, the long lines of the desired poem began to twine themselves in my mind. Having thought out all the stanzas, I said to myself, "I must get up and write these verses down, lest I fall asleep again and forget them."*

9   *So, with a sudden effort, I sprang out of bed, and found in the dimness an old stump of a pen which I remembered to have used the day before. I scrawled the verses almost without looking at the paper.*

Julia Ward Howe (1819–1910)

Union soldiers

10   *At this time, having completed my writing, I returned to bed and fell asleep, saying to myself, "I like this better than most things that I have written."*

11   The Union army had not been doing well in the war, and the soldiers were discouraged. The song "Battle Hymn of the Republic" inspired them to believe in themselves and what they were doing. The powerful words that Howe wrote described the Union army as good and honorable. She pictured the war as a struggle of good against evil.

12   Howe's story about writing the song also meant something to its listeners. She described the song as coming to her almost on its own. As a result, many people believed that her words were truly inspired.

13   "Battle Hymn of the Republic" became very popular in the Union army and throughout the North. It helped shape many Americans' ideas about why they were fighting. It encouraged them to believe that right was on their side.

14   The song made Julia Ward Howe famous. More important, though, it helped her reach her goal of supporting her country, in her own way.

15   After the Civil War was over, slavery was ended. Howe went on to work on other reforms, trying to make the world better in other ways. One very important reform was the fight for women's suffrage. In addition to working to get women the right to vote, Howe worked for peace, prison reform, and education reform.

16   Howe did not live to see women get the vote in 1920 or to see Mother's Day become an official holiday. Today, many people do not recognize her name. Just the same, American society is still touched by her work. The song "Battle Hymn of the Republic" still moves us as Americans. Perhaps most important is her example, which shows us that all people can find a way to help the causes they believe in and make a difference in the world.

from *Battle Hymn of the Republic*

Mine eyes have seen the glory of the coming of the Lord:
He is trampling out the vintage where the grapes of wrath are stored;
He hath loosed the fateful lightnings of His terrible swift sword:
His truth is marching on.

Comprehension Check

1. In paragraph 3, what does the word *abolition* mean?

   a. writing poetry and songs

   b. ending slavery

   c. making society better

   d. fighting in the Union army

2. When Julia Ward Howe mentions her *wont* (paragraph 8), she is talking about her

   a. tiredness from working hard.

   b. refusal to give up.

   c. usual way of behaving.

   d. desire to help others.

3. Compare the author's account with the words of Julia Ward Howe herself. What causes resulted in Howe's writing "Battle Hymn of the Republic"?

_____

_____

_____

_____

_____

_____

_____

_____

_____

4. Reread paragraphs 8–10. What information does Julia Ward Howe include in her description of writing "Battle Hymn of the Republic" that does not appear in the secondhand account in paragraph 6? How do these firsthand details affect you, as a reader?

_____

_____

_____

_____

_____

_____

_____

_____

_____

Compare and Contrast Texts

In this unit, you read about ways in which Americans have tried to make people's lives better. Think about what you have learned from the texts in this unit. Then choose two of the texts and compare and contrast how earlier Americans affected their own society and our society today. Which person or group did more to improve our society? Be prepared to discuss your ideas with the class.

Person or group:	Person or group:
Effect on their own society:	Effect on their own society:
Effect on society today:	Effect on society today:

The stronger effect on our society:

Return to the Essential Question

How can authors support their purpose in writing an informational text?

In small groups or as a class, discuss the Essential Question. Think about what you have learned about word meanings, text structures, and comparing and contrasting accounts. Use evidence from the four unit texts to answer the question.

LANGUAGE

Synonyms and Antonyms

Guided Instruction **Synonyms** are words with the same meaning or similar meanings. **Antonyms** are words with opposite meanings. Comparing a word with its synonyms and antonyms can help you understand what a word means.

Read this sentence from "Helping the Union": *At first, she thought that the idea was absurd—that in a war, only men could make a difference.*

Look at the chart to see examples of synonyms and antonyms of *absurd*.

| absurd | synonyms | *ridiculous, foolish* |
| | antonyms | *wise, reasonable* |

Guided Practice Write whether each word in parentheses is a synonym or antonym of the underlined word.

1. _____ . . . I approve much of your <u>conclusion</u>, that, in the meantime, we should draw all the good we can from this world. (judgment)

2. _____ . . . the reflection gave me more <u>chagrin</u> than the whistle gave me pleasure. (embarrassment)

3. _____ . . . neither had I the practical <u>deftness</u> which the preparing and packing of sanitary stores demanded. (awkwardness)

Independent Practice Write a synonym and an antonym for the underlined word in each sentence.

1. . . . when I was tempted to buy some <u>unnecessary</u> thing, . . .

_____

2. Instead, she found a <u>novel</u> way to help the Union cause.

_____

174 Unit 7 ■ Reading Informational Text: Craft and Structure

Copyright © by William H. Sadlier, Inc. All rights reserved.

Read the following passage in which vocabulary words, text structures, and different accounts appear. Then answer the questions on pages 175 and 176.

How Smallpox Was Defeated

(Genre: Explanatory Text)

1   Smallpox used to affect people all over the world. Many who got the disease died. The survivors often were left blind or horribly scarred.

2   In the early 1700s, a new treatment from China came to Europe. Doctors put ooze from a pox under the skin of a healthy person. This treatment was a primitive vaccine that safeguarded people against the disease.

3   In the American colonies, many were suspicious of the treatment. Benjamin Franklin was opposed at first. However, he became a supporter after his son died of smallpox. "In 1736 I lost one of my sons, a fine boy of four years old, by the small-pox . . . I long regretted bitterly, and still regret that I had not given it to him by inoculation." Later, a real smallpox vaccine was developed. Today, smallpox does not exist outside of laboratories.

Fill in the circle of the correct answer choice.

1. In paragraph 2, describing the vaccine as *primitive* means that it was

   ○ dangerous.

   ○ uncivilized.

   ○ simple.

   ○ not working.

2. What does the word *opposed* in paragraph 3 mean?

   ○ suspicious

   ○ fearful

   ○ supportive

   ○ against

3. What is an antonym of *suspicious* (paragraph 3)?

    ○ thoughtful   ○ jealous

    ○ confident   ○ horrified

4. In paragraph 2, what is a synonym for *safeguarded*?

    ○ protected   ○ predicted

    ○ warned   ○ tested

5. Underline the clues that tell you what this text is going to explain to readers.

6. Circle the firsthand account that appears in this explanatory text.

7. What problem did the people of the 1700s face? How was this problem solved?

    _____

    _____

8. How does this text's use of chronological order help you understand the fight against smallpox?

    _____

    _____

9. What could Benjamin Franklin not know about smallpox?

    _____

    _____

10. What is the effect on the reader of Benjamin Franklin's account of why he changed his mind?

    _____

    _____

Introducing UNIT 8

"What do you think?" "What's your opinion?" We often are asked to give an opinion on a topic. We often are asked to think about other people's opinions, too. In this unit about writing opinion pieces, you will learn how to present an opinion about a topic that is important to you.

To express an opinion effectively, you should have a clear statement at the beginning of the piece. You then should support that opinion with good reasons and with evidence—facts and details that show why your reasons make sense. A clear restatement of the opinion will help you end the piece well.

Your goal in writing an opinion piece is to convince the reader that your opinion is correct. Clear thinking—and, as always, correct grammar—will help make that happen.

Progress Check *Can I?*

Before Unit 8 / **After Unit 8**

- [ ] State an opinion clearly. [ ]
- [ ] Organize an opinion essay in a clear and appropriate fashion. [ ]
- [ ] Provide reasons supported by facts and details. [ ]
- [ ] Use formal and informal English correctly. [ ]
- [ ] Use frequently confused words correctly. [ ]
- [ ] Use helping verbs (modal auxiliaries) correctly. [ ]

HOME ✦ CONNECT...

In this unit, children will learn about writing pieces that **express an opinion** about a specific topic. Opinions come in many formats—editorials, TV commercials, political speeches, and more—so help your child recognize the various ways that opinions are expressed in the world around him or her.

As your child reads opinions on various topics, discuss why the writer is convincing. For example, guide your child to find a **clearly stated opinion**, **reasons that are supported by facts and details**, and **words and phrases that link the reasons to the opinion**. Then ask your child whether he or she agrees with the opinion and why (or why not).

Apply this discussion to your child's reading, as well. For example, ask your child his or her opinion about a story, poem, or book. You might even have him or her prepare an informal review and share it with the family.

Activity: Select an issue related to making the world a better place that is often discussed in your home or community or in the news. Have your child develop an opinion on the subject. Ask your child to think of reasons that support his or her position. Be sure to share your opinion, too, and to support it with strong reasons.

IN THIS UNIT, YOUR CHILD WILL...

- Learn to write opinion pieces about topics or texts, supporting his or her point of view with reasons and information.

- Build writing by introducing a topic clearly, stating an opinion, and then grouping related ideas together.

- Provide reasons that are supported by facts and details.

- Use appropriate words and phrases to link reasons to an opinion.

- Learn specific language skills:

  - Use formal or informal English, depending upon the situation.

  - Use frequently confused words (for example, *to/too/two, there/their*, and *whether/weather*) correctly.

  - Use modal auxiliary verbs (for example, *can, may,* and *must*) to express certain conditions.

WAYS TO HELP YOUR CHILD

Encourage your child to express opinions—and when he or she does so, listen to what he or she says. Ask questions about why your child holds this opinion. Ask about supporting details and information that help make his or her case.

> **ONLINE**
> **For more Home Connect activities, continue online at** sadlierconnect.com

Text Types and Purposes: Write Opinion Pieces

Essential Question:
How can I express and support my opinion in writing?

Write Opinion Pieces 180

Language: Formal and Informal English 184

Language: Frequently Confused Words 185

Language: Modal Auxiliaries 186

Speaking and Listening . . 188

Unit 8 Review 189

CREATING AN ORGANIZATIONAL STRUCTURE

Sanjay has used an outline to organize his editorial. It states his opinion, provides background information, gives three reasons that support his opinion, and ends with a conclusion.

Title: _____

I. Introduction
   a. Opinion: _____

   b. Background: _____
   _____
   _____
   _____

II. Supporting Reasons
   a. Reason 1: _____

   b. Reason 2: _____

   c. Reason 3: _____

III. Conclusion
   _____
   _____
   _____

TITLE

• Gets the reader thinking about the topic

INTRODUCTION

• Presents the topic and the writer's opinion

Underline the sentence that presents Sanjay's opinion.

Read a Student Model

Sanjay is a student in Ms. Lincoln's fourth-grade class. He has been asked to write an opinion piece that answers this question: *What is the most important invention of the past 100 years?* Sanjay has been asked to organize his writing and to support his point of view with reasons and information. As you read his essay, think about how you might support your point of view as you prepare to write your own opinion piece.

Martin Cooper holding a smartphone and the world's first mobile phone

The Most Important Invention

There have been many important inventions during the past 100 years. Advances in science and technology have made our lives better in many ways. New inventions allow doctors to diagnose and cure more illnesses. Engineers can build bigger, more efficient buildings. That said, the most important invention of the past 100 years is the smartphone.

Smartphones were developed from mobile phones. The first call on a mobile phone happened on April 3, 1973, when Martin Cooper placed a call on the Motorola company's new device in New York City.

The phone was 9 inches long, and it weighed 2.5 pounds. It had a talk time of 30 minutes, and it needed 10 hours to recharge the battery. Furthermore, the first mobile phones cost almost $4,000!

Technology has improved greatly since then. Today's smartphones are much lighter, have hours of battery life, and cost much less. It is their role in our lives today, however, that makes them so important.

The original mobile phone could only place and receive calls. Today's smartphones are important, first of all, because they can do much more. For example, the smartphone is a powerful computer. It allows me to send and receive e-mails and texts, as well as make and receive phone calls. I can use it to take pictures and videos and to play music and games—and it fits in the palm of my hand.

In addition, smartphones are very important because they make the latest technology available to almost anyone. According to a Nielsen survey, 114 million people in the United States, or 50.4 percent of the population, owned a smartphone in 2012. That number is rising all the time.

As a result of the smartphone's popularity, a new industry of creating applications, or apps, has risen. Some designers of popular apps have gone on to start successful companies.

LINKING WORDS AND PHRASES

- Use words and phrases to link the opinion to the reasons that support it.

Circle any linking words and phrases that you see on this page.

REASON 1:

- Provide strong reasons to support the opinion.
- Sanjay uses the phrase *first of all* to identify his first reason and to link it to his opinion.

REASON 2:

Underline the sentence that states Sanjay's second reason.

- Facts and details should support each reason.

Draw a box around the facts and details that support the second reason.

REASON 3:

Put a star by the sentence that states Sanjay's third reason.

CONCLUSION

Sanjay's conclusion restates his opinion, but in slightly different words. It also summarizes his reasons in an interesting way.

Underline the sentence that repeats Sanjay's opinion.

Finally, smartphones are especially important in emergencies. In a natural disaster, such as a hurricane, people often can use a smartphone to contact relatives and friends. Smartphone apps can help people find out about road closures and can direct people to emergency services. New apps are being developed to meet the rising demand for such help.

Nothing else can match the importance of the smartphone in today's world. People can use their smartphones to be in immediate contact, no matter who they are or where they are. They can do research and have fun with their smartphones, too. They might even use their smartphones to save lives! What great things this little device can do!

Use an outline like the one below to organize your own opinion essay about the development from the past 100 years that has had the greatest effect on your life. Then write a first draft of your essay on a separate sheet of paper. In your draft, be sure to support your reasons with facts and details and to use words and phrases to link those reasons to your opinion. You will use this draft to write your final essay in the Unit 8 Review section on page 190.

Title: _____

I. **Introduction**

   a. Opinion: _____

   _____

   b. Background: _____

   _____

   _____

   _____

II. **Supporting Reasons**

   a. Reason 1: _____

   _____

   b. Reason 2: _____

   _____

   c. Reason 3: _____

   _____

III. **Conclusion**

   _____

   _____

   _____

Formal and Informal English

Guided Instruction Written and spoken English can be formal or informal. Formal English is used when it is important to be "proper"—for example, when you are presenting an idea for a group to consider. Informal English is more casual. It is used in everyday conversations and communication—for example, when you are chatting with friends. Informal English uses contractions; formal English does not. In addition, the word choices and sentence structures in formal English often are more complicated than the ones in informal English.

- **Formal:** *Please notify Mr. Smith that his presence is required in the auditorium.*

- **Informal:** *Tell Mr. Smith that we need him in the auditorium.*

Guided Practice Identify each sentence as an example of **formal** or **informal** English.

1. The data indicate that the growth rate increases with the amount

   of sunlight. _____

2. When you get a chance, give me a call, OK? _____

3. What is the estimated time of your completion of the project?

   _____

4. When I saw them running toward me, hollering like crazy, I figured

   they were freaked about something. _____

Independent Practice Rewrite the first sentence so that it uses formal English. Rewrite the second sentence so that it uses informal English.

1. Great news! Your proposal won!

   _____

   _____

2. I am departing because I feel that this film is dull and cannot fulfill my demands for quality entertainment.

   _____

   _____

Frequently Confused Words

Guided Instruction Some words in English sound alike but have different spellings and different meanings. These words are called **homophones**. Here are some examples.

to (preposition indicating motion) **too** (also) **two** (a number)	**there** (in that place) **they're** (contraction for *they are*) **their** (belonging to them)
you're (contraction for *you are*) **your** (belonging to you)	**accept** (to receive or agree) **except** (preposition indicating leaving something out)
weather (what the climate is like) **whether** (if)	**hear** (to listen) **here** (in this place)

Guided Practice Underline the correct homophone in each sentence.

1. Aunt Lisa asked (weather / whether) we had eaten dinner.

2. They went to (they're / their / there) cabin for the weekend.

3. I want a treat, (too / two / to)!

Independent Practice Review the homophones in the chart. Then complete each sentence with the correct homophone.

1. I know _____ upset, but you should try to calm down.

2. Maylee likes every flavor _____ grapefruit.

3. After tryouts, Sam hoped that the team would _____ him as a member.

4. Did you _____ anything about what the _____ will be like on Saturday?

5. As a warm-up, I am going _____ run _____ laps around the track.

Modal Auxiliaries

Guided Instruction **Modal auxiliaries,** or helping verbs, are used with main verbs to express conditions. When a modal auxiliary is combined with the main verb, it creates a verb phrase.

Modal Auxiliary	Used to Express
can	ability
may	permission or possibility
must	strong belief or obligation
will	something that will happen in the future
should	the best action, which happens in past, present, or future

In the following sentence examples, the modal auxiliary is double-underlined and the main verb is underlined.

- *José <u>can</u> <u>sing</u> better than anyone else I know.*

   (José has great singing ability.)

- *Yes, you <u>may</u> <u>go</u> to the movies with Tanya's family.*

   (You have my permission to go.)

- *My keys <u>may</u> <u>be</u> in my coat pocket.*

   (My keys possibly are there—or they may be elsewhere.)

- *I <u>must</u> <u>tell</u> the truth about this.*

   (I strongly believe in being truthful.)

- *All students <u>must</u> <u>finish</u> their papers by Friday.*

   (The students have an obligation to do so.)

- *Keiko <u>will</u> <u>be</u> absent for the next three days.*

   (Her absence is in the future.)

- *We <u>should</u> <u>get</u> to school on time tomorrow.*

   (It would be good for us to do so.)

Guided Practice In each of the following sentences, underline the modal auxiliary. Then write what condition it expresses.

1. All band members must attend the rehearsal today. _____

2. Ben should finish his project by then. _____

3. Everyone who scored a 90 or better on the test may skip this homework assignment. _____

4. Elaine will watch that movie the day it opens. _____

5. Please, may I have a second helping? _____

Independent Practice Write your own sentences that express the conditions indicated.

1. Ability:

_____

_____

2. Permission:

_____

_____

3. Strong belief:

_____

_____

4. Best action:

_____

_____

5. Future happening:

_____

_____

Discuss the Essential Question

How can I express and support my opinion in writing?

Think about the Essential Question by responding to the questions below. Support your point of view with reasons, facts, and details.

1. What facts did the writer present to support his position about the most important invention of the past 100 years?

   _____

   _____

   _____

2. What are some phrases the writer used to link his opinion to reasons?

   _____

   _____

   _____

Use your notes above to discuss the Essential Question in small groups or as a class. Follow agreed-upon rules for discussion. Use the organizer below to record what you heard and how you participated.

Ideas I Agree or Disagree With		Questions I Asked
Agree		
Disagree		
New Ideas I Had During Discussion		**Questions I Answered**

This paragraph is written in informal English. It also has mistakes in homophones and modal auxiliaries. On the lines below, rewrite the paragraph so that it is correct and uses more formal English.

If you ask me, the coolest invention of the past 100 years will be the TV. Everybody needs TV programs to here stuff about news, whether, and politics. TV also must give us entertainment, allowing us to watch shows and movies whenever we feel like it. Without TV, their would be nothing too do.

Assignment: Write an opinion essay about the development of the past 100 years that has had the greatest effect on your life.

On the lines below, write the final copy of the opinion essay draft you created on page 183. Be sure you state your opinion clearly and develop your topic with reasons, facts, and details. Use linking words to connect your opinion and reasons, and provide a strong conclusion reinforcing your opinion. See the Writing Handbook (pages 275–283) for ways to improve your writing as you revise.

_____

_____

_____

_____

_____

_____

_____

_____

_____

_____

_____

_____

_____

_____

_____

_____

_____

_____

Introducing UNIT 9

Have you ever felt challenged in trying to achieve a goal? A challenge can be anything from overcoming a fear to solving a tough math problem to running a race. In this unit, you will see how characters in some works of traditional literature face challenges as they try to accomplish their goals or complete difficult journeys.

What is "traditional literature"? It is stories that have been handed down, generation after generation, for hundreds and even thousands of years. It includes some of our oldest stories: myths, folk tales, fables, legends, and epics. These kinds of stories are different in many ways, but they have much in common. They usually take place long ago and far away. They have fantastic elements, such as monsters, magical objects, and animals that talk. They have very basic kinds of characters: the hero, the villain, the princess, the trickster. They are often about heroes who are on a quest—an important personal journey marked by challenges that the hero has to face and overcome. Traditional literature also often has a moral, or lesson, for readers to understand and remember.

In this unit, you will learn to make connections between several very different examples of traditional literature.

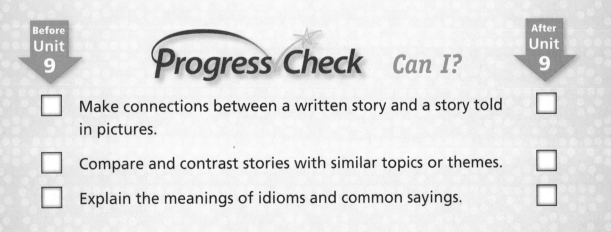

Before
Unit
9

Progress Check *Can I?*

After
Unit
9

- [ ] Make connections between a written story and a story told in pictures. [ ]

- [ ] Compare and contrast stories with similar topics or themes. [ ]

- [ ] Explain the meanings of idioms and common sayings. [ ]

HOME ✦ CONNECT...

IN THIS UNIT, YOUR CHILD WILL...

- Make connections between illustrations and the moments in the stories that the illustrations represent.

- Compare and contrast different kinds of texts that share a similar topic, theme, or pattern of events.

- Recognize and explain the meaning of common idioms, adages, and proverbs.

- Compare and contrast three texts on the same theme: the pairing of an epic and a graphic novel, the pairing of a folk tale and a fable, and a tall tale (legend).

Many children's books use illustrations to accent the text. Your child probably already has experience in **making connections between visuals and the text of a story**. Expand upon that experience by talking about examples in books, comic strips, and graphic novels. You also might use a print or online news story illustrated with a photograph or video clip to discuss the connection between the visual and the story events.

Stories told both in print and on film use **similar themes, topics, and patterns of events**. In movies, for example, many films focus on a young character on a heroic journey, accompanied by a variety of unusual characters. Suggest a topic (for example, good *vs.* evil), a theme (for example, the power of friendship), or a story pattern (for example, a quest). Then brainstorm with your child stories and films that contain it. Discuss why you think some of these themes, topics, and patterns of events appear in stories so often.

On the Go: Ask your child to make connections between everyday life and familiar stories. For example, you may have an interaction with someone who reminds your child of a character type (such as a wise older person), an event (such as a quest to reach a challenging personal goal), or a theme (such as taking a stand for what you believe is right). Ask your child to be as specific as he or she can. If the event connects with a favorite work of your own, share that with your child, too.

WAYS TO HELP YOUR CHILD

Encourage your child's imagination and speaking skills by inviting him or her to create and share original stories. These stories may be inspired in various ways, but the topic and plot of each one should be clear. Ask questions that encourage your child to think about each story's theme and to explore connections that the story may have to other stories that he or she has enjoyed.

ONLINE

For more Home Connect activities, continue online at sadlierconnect.com

Reading Literature: Integration of Knowledge and Ideas

Essential Question:
What can readers learn by making connections between literary works?

Making Connections Between Texts 194

Comparing and Contrasting
Themes and Topics 200

Close Reading 206

Connect Across Texts 211

Language: Idioms, Adages, and Proverbs 212

Unit 9 Review 213

WORDS TO KNOW

declined

oppressed

tyrant

A **story** can be presented in **text**, in **visuals**, or in **both**. The visual version will **depict details** from the text version.

CITE EVIDENCE

A In traditional literature, such as an epic, characters are often described in broad, general terms. They are "kind" or "cunning" or "wise." In paragraph 1, Gilgamesh is described as "a powerful king." Circle another phrase in paragraph 1 that describes Gilgamesh. Can you think of a character from another story or from real life who could be described in the same way?

B Underline an action that Ishtar takes in paragraph 4. What does Panel 3 of the graphic novel show about this moment that the text does not include? Which version of this scene do you think is more dramatic?

Gilgamesh's Quest for Immortality

(Genre: Sumerian Epic)

1   Once upon a time, long ago and far away in the ancient land of Sumer, there was a powerful king named Gilgamesh who was part human and part divine. He ruled the great city of Uruk, which was walled in on all sides. Gilgamesh was an imposing **tyrant** and ruled with an iron fist. He **oppressed** the people of Uruk without remorse. It was a terrible time to live in Uruk.

2   The people prayed and prayed, and their prayers were finally answered. The goddess Aruru took some clay and threw it onto the ground. A huge, hairy beast of a man rose from the clay. His name was Enkidu, and he was created to challenge Gilgamesh and free Uruk from the tyrannical king's clutches.

3   But something else happened. Over time, Gilgamesh and Enkidu became great friends—best friends, in fact. They were inseparable. City dwellers were struck by the contrast of their gleaming, statuesque king and his wild companion. The two fought many battles together.

4   After one especially tough fight, Gilgamesh washed himself and placed his crown atop his head. At that moment, he was so stunningly handsome that the goddess Ishtar proposed marriage to him. He **declined** her offer, and Ishtar, humiliated, flew into a rage and vowed revenge on Gilgamesh.

5   Ishtar knew how to punish Gilgamesh. Summoning her powers, she ordered the earth to open up and swallow Enkidu. Instantly, Gilgamesh's beloved friend was gone forever, their bond permanently broken.

CITE EVIDENCE

C A **visual presentation** of a story shows specific details from the text. How does Panel 1 of the **graphic novel** show that Gilgamesh is a "tyrant"? Draw a box around the part of the panel that illustrates how Gilgamesh's way of ruling affects his people. Explain whether the graphic novel or the text provides a more vivid idea of how Gilgamesh rules.

D The text says that Enkidu and Gilgamesh became best friends. Draw a box around where this is indicated visually in Panel 2. What other details are included in this panel that are not in the text? Why does the graphic novel version presents the scene in this way?

Comprehension Check

Compare and contrast the text version to the panels from the graphic novel version. What details from the text version appear in the graphic novel? What additional details are provided? How does the visual version help your understanding of the story?

Guided Practice

Gilgamesh's Quest for Immortality *continued*

WORDS TO KNOW

collapse

treacherous

volume

CITE EVIDENCE

A Circle the text that matches Panel 1 on this page. How does the illustration reflect the written description?

B Underline the text that connects to the scene in Panel 2. Discuss with a partner: In a complete version of this graphic novel, should several panels be devoted to details of the sea journey, or would it be more important to get quickly to the meeting with Faraway?

6   Upon learning of his friend's death, Gilgamesh let out a long, painful wail. Its **volume** was deafening. He pulled out his hair and tore at his clothes.

7   "What am I to do?" Gilgamesh cried. "My best friend is lost to me forever!" He wandered the woods for days, determined to avoid Enkidu's fate. At last he decided, "I must find a way to live forever, in case Ishtar will come for me next. I shall seek the man called 'Faraway.'"

8   Gilgamesh set out alone on a long, difficult journey. He traveled along a **treacherous** mountain pass, past two gruesome scorpion-men, through a tunnel under the mountains themselves, and finally to a ferryman who could guide him across the sea. After chopping down a tree to make a boat rudder, Gilgamesh was on the verge of **collapse**. But he and the ferryman finally began the 45-day journey across the sea.

9   Despite rough seas and high winds, Gilgamesh arrived at the place he was seeking. The man called Faraway was standing on the shore, waiting.

10   "I wish never to die," Gilgamesh told him.

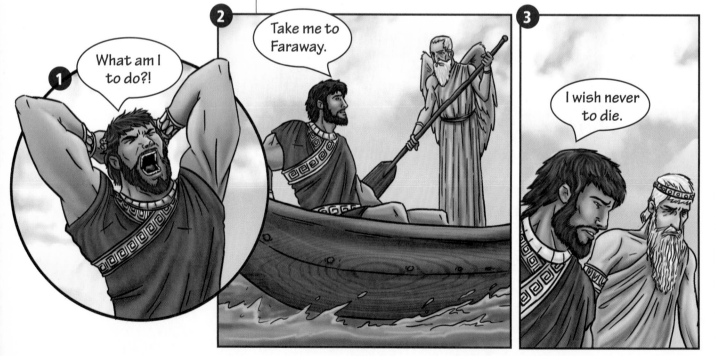

11   "That is impossible," the man replied, "for death is a mystery, and it must come to us all."

12   But Gilgamesh pleaded with him, describing his journey and his friend Enkidu. Faraway was moved—and, more important, he was convinced.

Comprehension Check

1. What does it mean that Faraway was "convinced" by Gilgamesh's story?

    a. He believed that Gilgamesh should know the secret of living forever.

    b. He believed that Gilgamesh had gone to a lot of trouble to see him.

    c. He believed that Gilgamesh truly missed his friend Enkidu.

    d. He believed that Gilgamesh had been badly treated by Ishtar.

2. If there were a panel after Panel 3, what would it probably show?

    a. Gilgamesh looking toward the ferryman and saying, "I want to go home to my city of Uruk."

    b. Gilgamesh looking at Faraway and saying, "Death is a mystery, isn't it?"

    c. Faraway looking at Gilgamesh and saying, "That is not possible, for death must come to us all."

    d. Gilgamesh saying, "I'm looking for a man called 'Faraway.'"

3. With a partner, discuss which visuals you think best connect with the text. Point out text details as you talk. Then choose one panel and tell how you might have drawn and written it differently.

_____

_____

MAKING CONNECTIONS BETWEEN TEXTS

Independent Practice

Gilgamesh's Quest for Immortality *continued*

WORDS TO KNOW

immensely

retrieve

transformed

CITE EVIDENCE

A Underline the sentence in paragraph 14 that connects with Panel 1. How does the action remind you of other brave actions you have read about, seen in movies, or know about?

B In paragraph 15, circle the detail shown in Panel 2. Then discuss whether this was a good detail to show in the graphic novel.

13   The wise man revealed a secret to Gilgamesh. "It is a prickly plant that you seek," began Faraway, "and it lives at the bottom of the sea. **Retrieve** it, and you can be **transformed**. It will grant you anything you desire."

14   Gilgamesh tied rocks to his feet and threw himself into the sea. Underwater, he saw the thorny plant and snatched it up. **Immensely** satisfied, Gilgamesh held the plant protectively in his hand.

15   Gilgamesh rejoined the ferryman to prepare to sail home. He could think of nothing but his wish and how he would be able to live forever. But it was not to be. For when they stopped at a natural spring for a drink, and Gilgamesh was not looking, a serpent stole the plant away and ate it. Gilgamesh cried out as the snake's old skin began to shed away, revealing a new skin underneath. The serpent had received the plant's gift.

16   Gilgamesh could only cry, "I have failed! I shall never be immortal!" And with that, Gilgamesh sailed home to the walled city of Uruk, his kingdom, mourning his lost friend and what might have been.

Comprehension Check   MORE ONLINE **sadlierconnect.com**

1. In some cultures, the story of the snake and the plant could be told in a legend of its own. If that legend were told, what would it explain?

   a. why snakes shed their skin

   b. why snakes are considered dangerous

   c. why snakes live forever

   d. why some snakes are poisonous

2. Which line from the story would be very difficult to present using only visuals?

   a. "Gilgamesh tied rocks to his feet. . . . "

   b. "Underwater, he saw the thorny plant and snatched it up."

   c. "Gilgamesh could think of nothing but his wish. . . . "

   d. " . . . a serpent stole the plant away from him."

3. You have seen only a few panels from a graphic novel version of the epic of Gilgamesh. Which other incidents mentioned in the text would you expect to be presented in a full graphic novel? Are there any parts of the text that could be left out of a graphic novel presentation? Cite details in your answers.

   _____

   _____

   _____

   _____

Guided Instruction

WORDS TO KNOW

challenge

devoted

griddle

labored

It is useful to **compare and contrast** the **themes, topics,** and **patterns of events** in traditional literature.

CITE EVIDENCE

A The **topic** of many folk tales involves a clash between enemies. Finn MacCool is a hero in this story. Find and underline the name of the villain. What villains can you remember from other stories, TV shows, or movies? Based on your knowledge, what do you think this villain might do?

B Traditional works of literature have common **patterns**. In one pattern, called the quest tale, a hero goes on a journey and has adventures along the way. Another pattern is the trickster tale, in which a clever character outsmarts a villain. Underline a clue in paragraph 10 that suggests this story might be a trickster tale.

Finn MacCool and Oonagh

(Genre: Irish Folk Tale)

1   Long ago, in the beautiful land of Ireland, there lived a giant named Finn MacCool. Finn was enormous and strong, and all day long he worked alongside his giant friends, building a bridge to Scotland. As he **labored** away, his wife was never far from his mind. Oonagh was her name, and Finn was **devoted** to her.

2   They lived together at the very top of tall Knockmany Hill. It was quite a climb to get home every night, and there was never a break from the howling Irish winds. Yet there was a method to Finn's madness: The top of Knockmany Hill was a perfect look-out perch.

3   You see, there was a certain giant in the land who was to be avoided. His name was Cucullin, and although Cucullin prided himself on being the strongest giant of them all, there was one individual he had never dared **challenge**: Finn MacCool. Finn was well aware of this, and that's why he built his home on top of Knockmany Hill, for up there, he would be able to see if Cucullin was coming for him. He knew that day would come.

4   One day, Finn took a break from his work and decided to go home and see his beloved Oonagh.

5   He trekked up the hill and met Oonagh, who gave him a loving tap on his cheek.

6   "Ah, welcome home, ya darlin' rogue," Oonagh smiled, "but what's botherin' ya? I can see't on y'face."

7   "It's Cucullin that's troublin' me," Finn replied, "I believe he's comin' for me."

8   Finn, you see, had a special talent: When he stuck his thumb into his mouth and sucked on it, he could see the future.

9   "Sure enough, he'll come today," Finn mumbled, his thumb in his mouth.

10   "Piece of cake, my darlin' Finn," Oonagh winked. "I've got a plan to hatch."

11   Finn was relieved: His beloved Oonagh was clever, and she had bailed him out before.

12   Oonagh raced down the hill and went to all of her neighbors, asking for their iron **griddles**. After collecting twenty griddles, she returned home, ground them up, and made griddle cakes—some with iron and some without. This was all she needed to do, so she sat with Finn and they waited.

CITE EVIDENCE

C The **theme**, or main idea, of a folk tale is often a moral, or lesson. There are clues to the moral throughout a folk tale. There is a clue in paragraph 10: Oonagh will help Finn. Circle two details in paragraph 11 that show why we might call Oonagh helpful.

D Characters in folk tales may have strange abilities and take strange actions. When Finn sucks his thumb, he can see the future. In paragraph 12, put a star next to the strange action Oonagh takes. What do you think she is doing?

Comprehension Check

Think about what you have read so far.

Does this story have a theme or characters similar to any other stories you have read? Explain, citing specific examples.

COMPARING/CONTRASTING THEMES AND TOPICS

Guided Practice

Finn MacCool and Oonagh *continued*

WORDS TO KNOW

concede

derived

perplexed

CITE EVIDENCE

A Put a star by the strange action that Oonagh wants Finn to take. Explain how you know that this is part of Oonagh's plan and that Finn does not know what the plan is.

B Underline the sentence that tells you how Cucullin gets his strength. With a partner, discuss how Cucullin and Finn are alike and different.

13   At 2 o'clock, Finn spied Cucullin climbing up the hill.

14   "All right," Oonagh whispered to Finn, "put on these baby clothes and climb into the crib."

15   Finn looked **perplexed**, but he trusted her.

16   "I'm looking for Finn MacCool," Cucullin bellowed when he saw Oonagh.

17   "I'm sorry, but he's not here," she replied. "He just went off to slay the giant Cucullin."

18   "What? That's *me* you're talkin' about, and I'm here to slay *him*," he exclaimed.

19   "Well, he's not here, but you can wait for him—and maybe you could help me with a few things that he usually does," Oonagh began. "On blustery days like today, he turns the house away from the wind. Would you mind?"

20   "I can do that!" Cucullin bragged. You see, Cucullin had a unique talent as well: He **derived** all his strength from his third finger. So he went outside and, with only his third finger, turned the house.

21   "Thank you," Oonagh said. "You must be hungry, so eat these griddle cakes I've prepared. They're Finn's favorite, but he won't mind."

22   "Griddle cakes!" Cucullin cried. "They're my favorite!" He grabbed two of them and stuffed them into his mouth. "Aaargh!" he screamed. "I've broken my teeth! What are these cakes made of?"

23   "They're just my regular recipe. My baby son loves them, too," Oonagh said as she handed a griddle cake without iron to the boy in the crib (who was Finn disguised as a baby, of course). The "baby" gobbled up the griddle cake easily.

24 Cucullin was stunned. "Why, if the baby can eat those cakes, he must be incredibly strong!"

25 "You can say that again," Oonagh agreed, "but the boy is not nearly as strong as his father."

26 With that, Cucullin changed his mind. "Well," he mused, "I will **concede** defeat and say that Finn MacCool must be the strongest giant of all. But may I inspect this extraordinary boy's teeth?"

27 "You may," Oonagh replied.

Comprehension Check

1. How is Ishtar from the story of Gilgamesh different from Oonagh?

(a.) Ishtar is very foolish and Oonagh is clever.

b. Ishtar works against the man she loves, but Oonagh helps Finn.

c. Ishtar is mortal but Oonagh is a goddess.

d. Ishtar seems trustworthy and Oonagh is untrustworthy.

2. In "Gilgamesh's Quest for Immortality," Gilgamesh wanted to find a way to live forever. In "Finn MacCool and Oonagh," Finn and Oonagh want to find

(a.) the perfect recipe for griddle cakes.

b. a way to make friends with the giant Cucullin.

c. a way to keep their house from blowing away.

d. a way to keep Cucullin from challenging Finn.

3. So far in the story, how are Oonagh and Cucullin different? Work with a partner, and be sure to cite text evidence.

cause one of them help people.

_____

_____

Independent Practice

Finn MacCool and Oonagh *continued*

CITE EVIDENCE

A Draw a circle around the **theme** or moral of "Finn MacCool and Oonagh." What kind of real-life situation might demonstrate the same theme?

B Draw a circle around the moral of the fable "The Fox and the Snail." What is another way to state this moral?

28 As Cucullin peered into the boy's mouth, Finn saw his chance and bit down hard on Cucullin's special third finger. Cucullin screamed in pain.

29 "That'll teach you, Cucullin! Now, hit the road!" Oonagh shouted. "And don't ever come back!"

30 Cucullin raced down the hill, never to be seen or heard from again.

31 Finn took off the baby clothes and hugged his wife in gratitude. She had taught him a lesson: Brains are better than **brawn**.

The Fox and the Snail

(**Genre:** Swiss Fable)

32 One warm summer's day, a wily fox was resting by the meadow. He saw a snail on the ground next to him. "How slow and stupid snails are," he thought. And immediately an idea came to him. He proposed a wager as to which of them could reach town more quickly.

33 "You're on!" said the snail, and he set out immediately. The snail traveled slowly, for he was carrying his house on his back, as was his **custom**.

34 The fox continued his rest, intending to start off in the cool of the evening, and he dozed off. The snail quickly took advantage of this **circumstance** and crept into the fox's thick, bushy tail. As evening approached, the fox took off, surprised that the snail was nowhere to be seen.

35   When he reached the town gate but still could see nothing of the snail, the fox turned around and called out **tauntingly**, "Snail, pick up your pace! I can't wait months for you to get here!"

36   "I'm already here!" answered the snail. Without being seen, he had rolled out of the fox's tail and through the bottom of the gate.

37   Thus the fox had to admit it: Pride is no match for cleverness.

Comprehension Check

(MORE ONLINE) **sadlierconnect.com**

1. Compare what you read about patterns in traditional literature with what you have seen in "Finn MacCool and Oonagh" and "The Fox and the Snail." What similar pattern of events do these stories share?

   a. They both have unusual characters.

   b. They both have simple plots and a clearly stated moral.

   c. They both deal with a trick that is played on a strong opponent.

   d. They both deal with the pattern of the quest, or journey.

2. Which word best describes both Oonagh and the snail?

   a. proud

   b. intelligent

   c. gloomy

   d. honest

3. How are the themes of the folk tale about Finn MacCool and this animal fable similar? How are they different? Be sure to discuss the moral of each story.

Becouse one is intelligen and the other is helpful

Pecos Bill and Slue-Foot Sue

(Genre: Tall Tale/Legend)

1   Maybe you've heard of Pecos Bill. He was the roughest, toughest fella who ever lived in the American Wild West. Legend has it that Pecos Bill was born around the time that Texas was discovered, which was in the early 1830s.

2   Even as a boy, Bill showed he was a tough kid when he brought home a bear as a playmate. His mother could only roll her eyes and smile. She was a tough woman herself: She was sturdy and strict, and she wasn't afraid to fight off big snakes with her broom handle.

3   Bill's family moved farther west when he was a boy. During the journey, their wagon crossed the Pecos River and Bill fell out; but because Bill had sixteen brothers and sisters, no one noticed that he was missing.

4   Bill watched the wagon ride off into the distance. But he wasn't sad; he just shrugged and started to walk. After a while, he met a mother coyote who offered to take him in and raise him as her own. Bill gladly accepted.

5   As a member of the pack, Bill learned to do many things. He yipped and yelped at the moon, scratched his itchy fleas, and learned to hunt.

6   One day, when Bill was a teenager, a cowhand came along and, upon seeing Bill, froze in his tracks. It was one of Bill's long-lost brothers. Bill said to him that it was impossible for them to be related—he was a coyote!

7   "That's nonsense," his brother replied, "for you don't have a tail!"

8   Since Bill's brother had a point, Bill left the coyotes and went home.

9 Reunited with his family, Bill learned to live the life of a cowhand. His brother taught him many new skills, and soon enough Bill showed extraordinary abilities. He taught broncos how to buck, and he invented the branding iron and cattle roping. He also invented the tarantula and the centipede—just so he could have something to fool his pals with. In his spare time, he dug the Rio Grande. He just always kept busy.

10 The day came when Bill needed new challenges, so he said goodbye to his family and set out, atop his horse, on his own.

11 Bill came upon a trapper one day and asked him where the toughest men resided, for he wanted to live among them. The trapper was hesitant to reply, so Bill glared at him until he spilled the beans.

12 "Go farther west," the trapper said. So Bill did just that.

13 He galloped along on his horse for many days until one day, when the animal bruised her hoof and could not go any farther. Once more, Bill was on his own, but it didn't bother him.

14 Bill grabbed the saddle and walked for miles until he came upon a large rattlesnake, who hissed at him threateningly and reared up. Bill yawned and allowed the snake three bites before wrestling it to the ground.

15 The snake cried for mercy, and Bill let go. Then Bill met a cougar that looked as if it weighed a ton. As he did with the snake, Bill humored the animal, wrestling it to the ground and chuckling to himself as he did it. Legend says that the fur of the cougar flew so high that it made a cloud that blocked out the sun. Bill slapped his saddle on the cougar, threw the snake over his shoulder, and rode off.

16 That evening he came upon a group of cowhands sitting around a campfire and looking mighty tough and mean. They eyed him suspiciously, even though he was riding an enormous cougar and carrying a rattlesnake.

17 Bill—not being able to help who he was—grabbed their pot of hot coffee and drank it down in one gulp. Then he downed a kettle full of beans and washed them down with another pot of coffee. The leader of the lot stood up, eyed Bill, and said, "Stranger, I was the boss here; but you're the boss now."

18   Bill stayed with the cowhands and learned that he now was in Arizona. The first thing he did was find a new horse, Widowmaker. He fed her sticks of dynamite until she was strong and feisty enough for him to ride.

19   One day, a raging tornado came barreling across the land. It was as wide as a state and as loud as ten thousand freight trains. A more terrible tornado had never been seen, everyone agreed.

20   Bill took one look at that tornado and knew that he could tame it. Just as it came roaring toward him, he leaped on top of it, riding it like a bucking bronco. His big hat flopped in the fierce winds, but Bill never let go. He rode that storm for miles across Arizona until finally it dissolved into rain, washing out the entire Grand Canyon. As the storm broke down, it tossed Pecos Bill off like a sack of potatoes, and his hard landing in the southern California desert created Death Valley.

21   Pecos Bill was not alone his entire life. He did meet a special gal named Slue-Foot Sue. Sue was no slouch of a rider herself; in fact, she had a reputation for being able to stay on the most spirited bronco.

22   When Bill first set eyes on Sue, he instantly fell in love—and she felt the same way. They were two of a kind, and they were meant to be together.

23   Bill was a unique guy, but Sue had her own peculiarities. One of them was that she loved riding giant catfish—as big as whales—down the Rio Grande.

24   Something else that Sue loved was Widowmaker, Bill's horse. On their wedding day, Sue—still wearing her wedding dress—climbed onto Widowmaker and rode her for hours. Sue's wedding dress had a springy bustle in the back, so as she rode, she bounced. Unfortunately, she kept bouncing and couldn't stop. Finally, Bill had to knock her down out of the sky so she could get something to eat!

25   For all his toughness, Pecos Bill was really a pretty nice guy.

26   Once, a cowhand who was riding Widowmaker was tossed so high that he landed on the top of Pikes Peak in Colorado. Bill rescued the man by roping him around the shoulders and dragging him down the mountain.

27   There was another story about a new fence. Holes in the ground were needed to secure the fence, so Bill had an idea: He asked the prairie dogs in the area if they would like to dig the holes.

28   The prairie dogs loved being helpful, and the men loved not having to do the tedious work of digging the holes.

Who but Bill would care what a prairie dog liked or how it felt?

29   Just how Pecos Bill died is a mystery. Cowhands tell various tales, but the most widely believed story is that Bill (who, don't forget, was the roughest, toughest fella in the West, and maybe anywhere) loved stirring nails, fishhooks, and barbed wire into his food for added flavor and texture. All those nails and whatnot rusted inside of him and eventually killed him, which is what bad habits can do.

30   Pecos Bill was mourned, but he was never forgotten.

Comprehension Check

1. The legend of Pecos Bill is called a tall tale. One topic in many legends is telling the origin of something in nature. According to this legend, Bill created Death Valley. What other origin tale have you read in this unit?

   a. how Pecos Bill created Pikes Peak in this tall tale

   b. why the snake sheds its skin in the legend of Gilgamesh

   c. how the snail won the race in the Swiss fable

   d. why griddle cakes are made with iron in the Irish folk tale

2. The relationship between Pecos Bill and Slue-Foot Sue is most like which other relationship that you have read about in this unit?

   a. Gilgamesh and Ishtar

   b. Finn MacCool and Cucullin

   c. Finn MacCool and Oonagh

   d. the fox and the snail

3. Review the visuals that go along with this story. Identify some details from the visuals that connect with text details. Then tell how the visuals help you better understand and enjoy the story.

Pecos bill was tough kid and he brong a bear in his house, And he used the bear has his playmate, And bill got married with sue and on their wedding got bill horse and she was riding it, It helped me understand and enjoy that bill like having playmate's and animals.

4. Think about "Pecos Bill and Slue-Foot Sue" and "Finn MacCool and Oonagh." How are these stories similar? How are they different? Consider the characteristics of traditional literature, and be sure to cite specifics from the text in your answer.

Compare and Contrast Texts

In this unit, you read different kinds of stories from traditional literature. Think about the ways in which these stories are similar and different. Then use the Venn diagram below to compare and contrast two of the stories. List key details and important points from the texts to show the similarities and differences between them. Be prepared to discuss your ideas with your class.

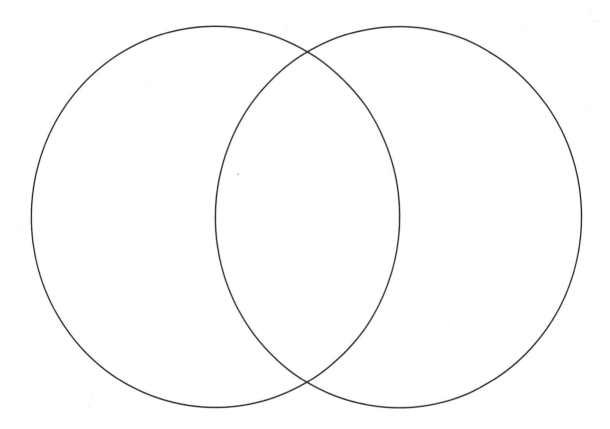

Return to the Essential Question

What can readers learn by making connections between literary works?

In small groups or as a class, discuss the Essential Question. Think about what you have learned from comparing these works' themes, morals, and common patterns. Use evidence from the three texts to answer the question.

Idioms, Adages, and Proverbs

Guided Instruction Works of traditional literature sometimes use special expressions such as idioms or proverbs to help tell their stories. An **idiom** is a common everyday expression whose meaning is different from the literal meaning of its words. For example, when the snail tells the fox, "You're on!" he is using an idiom that means "I agree."

A **proverb** (sometimes called an **adage**) is a short statement or saying that expresses a common truth. A fable's moral or lesson is often stated as a proverb. For example, the moral of the famous story "The Tortoise and the Hare" is stated in the proverb "Slow and steady wins the race." In "Finn MacCool and Oonagh," the proverb "Brains are better than brawn" states the moral of the story.

Guided Practice Write whether each expression is an *idiom* or a *proverb*. Remember that an idiom is an everyday expression and a proverb is a short saying that states a truth or gives advice.

1. "the early bird gets the worm" _____

2. "hit the road" _____

3. "piece of cake" _____

4. "look before you leap" _____

5. "washed them down" _____

Independent Practice Rewrite these statements from "Finn MacCool and Oonagh" in your own words.

1. Brains are better than brawn. (proverb)

_____

_____

2. Yet there was a method to Finn's madness. . . . (idiom)

_____

_____

Read the following two works of traditional literature. Think about what they have in common with other traditional stories. Then answer the questions on pages 213 and 214.

The Mother and the Wolf

(Genre: Aesop's Fable)

1   A famished Wolf was prowling outside a cottage when he heard a Child weeping inside; then he heard the Mother say, "Stop crying, Child, or I will give you to the Wolf!" The thought of such a wonderful gift caused the Wolf to wait there, under an open window, all day.

2   Toward nightfall, he heard the Mother's voice again: "Child, the Wolf shall not get you because Daddy will kill him if he should come near!" It was a bitter pill for the Wolf to swallow.

3   So, do not believe everything you hear.

The Hawk and the Squirrel

(Genre: Filipino Folk Tale)

4   Hawk sat in a tree, eating a salty fish, while hungry Squirrel spied the scene from below and then called out, "Hawk! Sing to me with your voice so soft and sweet!"

5   Filled with pride, Hawk began to sing, and the fish fell to the ground. Adding insult to injury, Squirrel grabbed it and ran away. Do not always believe what others tell you.

Fill in the circle of the correct answer choice.

1. Which of these is a moral?

   ○ ...the Wolf shall not get you...

   ○ . . . it was a bitter pill. . . .

   ○ . . . Squirrel grabbed it and ran away.

   ○ So, do not believe everything you hear.

2. What does the idiom *adding insult to injury* mean?

   ○ causing harm to someone

   ○ saying something cruel

   ○ making the situation worse

   ○ winning the victory

3. Which characters are defeated by trickery in these tales?

   ○ Wolf and Hawk   ○ Squirrel and Mother

   ○ Mother and Child   ○ Hawk and Squirrel

4. Which characteristic of traditional literature appears in both tales?

   ○ A character goes on a quest.   ○ The characters do strange things.

   ○ The stories take place long ago. ○ There is a clearly stated moral.

5. Underline the name of the character who is the villain in the first story.

6. Circle the theme, or moral, of the second story.

7. What is one way that you can tell the second story is traditional literature?

   _____

   _____

8. Which character in the second tale is like the Mother in the first tale? Why?

   _____

   _____

9. Suppose that you could represent the second story with just one picture. What would the picture be? Why?

   _____

   _____

   _____

10. How are the themes, or morals, of the two stories similar and different? Explain.

   _____

   _____

   _____

Introducing UNIT 10

In this unit about scientific quests for knowledge, you will learn how to write a research report, a type of informative or explanatory text based on evidence.

Before writing a research report, you must choose a topic and gather information about it. When writing, you use the evidence you gathered to support your ideas about the topic. Even though you are writing about facts, you want your research report to be interesting and believable. So, you cite relevant evidence from both print and digital sources.

To be effective, a research report must be well organized, grouping related information in sections. Summaries and explanations of events should be clear and concise, and the writing should be grammatically correct, with correct capitalization and spelling. The report should end with a list of sources.

Progress Check   Can I?

Before Unit 10 / **After Unit 10**

☐ Write a research report that investigates a topic. ☐

☐ Gather relevant evidence from print and digital sources. ☐

☐ Take notes and organize the information logically. ☐

☐ Present the information in a way that builds knowledge. ☐

☐ Provide a list of sources. ☐

☐ Write using commas in compound sentences correctly. ☐

☐ Write using correct capitalization. ☐

☐ Write using correct spelling. ☐

HOME✦CONNECT...

In this unit, children will learn about writing a **research report**. A research report is a type of text that explains or informs. Explain to your child that it tells the reader about a topic that the writer has researched—that is, a topic about which the writer has **gathered facts and evidence**. Point out that a research report can be about a science topic, a social studies topic, a famous person, or any other topic that interests a writer.

Guide your child as he or she practices researching a topic, using both **print and digital sources**. Encourage your child to write down facts and evidence about a specific topic in a chart or on note cards. Help your child **categorize the evidence** by color-coding the chart or grouping the note cards. Explain that he or she needs to **include source information** for each fact or piece of evidence collected. Source information includes the title of the source, the author, the publication, and the date published.

Conversation Starter: Explain to your child that researching a topic and writing a report about it is not just a challenge; it is an opportunity to build knowledge on the topic. Ask: *What topic do you want to know more about? What do you think you can learn about the topic by researching it? Where can you find facts and evidence about the topic?*

IN THIS UNIT, YOUR CHILD WILL...

- Learn to write a research report that includes an introduction, develops subtopics with evidence, and ends with a concluding statement or section.

- Gather relevant information from relevant print and digital sources by taking notes and categorizing the information.

- Learn specific language skills and apply them:

  - Use commas correctly in compound sentences.

  - Use correct capitalization.

  - Correctly spell frequently misspelled words.

  - Consult a dictionary for the correct spelling of a word.

WAYS TO HELP YOUR CHILD

Remind your child that it is important to use credible, or trustworthy, sources when doing research. Point out that Internet sites with URLs that end in .edu (education websites) and .gov (government websites) are usually credible sources. Information found at a .com website, however, is not always credible, so it should be verified by another source.

ONLINE

For more Home Connect activities, continue online at sadlierconnect.com

Research to Build and Present Knowledge: Write Research Reports

Essential Question:
How can I develop a topic into a research report?

Write Research Reports 218

Language: Commas in
Compound Sentences. 223

Language: Capitalization 224

Language: Spelling 225

Speaking and Listening. 226

Unit 10 Review 227

CREATING AN ORGANIZATIONAL STRUCTURE

Marcus used an outline to organize his research report. It has an introduction, three subtopic sections, and a conclusion.

Title: _____
  I. **Introduction**
      a. Topic: _____
      b. Background: _____
      _____
      _____
  II. **Subtopic 1:** _____
      a. Fact: _____
      b. Fact: _____
 III. **Subtopic 2:** _____
      a. Fact: _____
      b. Fact: _____
 IV. **Subtopic 3:** _____
      a. Fact: _____
      b. Fact: _____
  V. **Conclusion**
      _____
      _____
      _____

TITLE

- Identifies the topic for the reader

INTRODUCTION

- Introduces the research topic
- Gives background
- States the different aspects of the topic the writer has investigated

Underline the sentence that states the different aspects of the topic the writer has investigated.

Read a Student Model

Marcus is a student in Ms. Hanson's fourth-grade class. He has been asked to write a research report on a scientific quest. A quest is an exploration in search of knowledge. Marcus must gather, summarize, and explain relevant information from both print and digital sources. As you read his research report, think about what you will research and how you will organize, summarize, and explain the information you gather for your own research report about a real-life quest.

Exploring Mars

The planet Mars is millions of miles away from Earth. Yet, in their quest for knowledge about the planet, scientists on Earth are able to explore Mars. They do so through remote-controlled rovers. The most recent rover sent to Mars is called <u>Curiosity</u>. Like other rovers, <u>Curiosity</u> has no people on board. Scientists control it from Earth. The National Aeronautics and Space Administration (NASA) launched <u>Curiosity</u> on November 26, 2011. The rover landed on Mars on August 6, 2012. NASA is exploring Mars for several reasons: to learn if life ever existed on Mars, to learn more about the planet's atmosphere and geology, and to learn if people can be sent to Mars.

Signs of Water

Soon after landing on Mars, <u>Curiosity</u> filmed a dried-up streambed and detected clay minerals. Scientists wondered if these minerals could be from a dried-up lake. Based on these and other discoveries, NASA announced that Mars could have supported germ-like life long ago. The scientist in charge of the mission said, "We have found a habitable environment."

Atmosphere and Geology

<u>Curiosity</u> has made several important findings about Mars's atmosphere and geology, too. The rover collected data on radiation. Scientists concluded from the data that the radiation in Mars's atmosphere is the same as that of the International Space Station. <u>Curiosity</u> also found oxygen, hydrogen, and carbon in a rock sample. These chemicals are also signs that Mars could have once supported life.

Humans on Mars

<u>Curiosity</u> has also helped NASA get closer to sending humans to Mars. NASA landed <u>Curiosity</u> on Mars with a crane that was attached to another spacecraft. Before this time, rovers were dropped on Mars. According to Rebecca Boyle of <u>Popular Science</u> magazine, previous rovers released airbags to land on. Then they bounced around. That sort of landing would be very hard on humans, but the crane-type landing is much smoother.

SUBTOPIC 1

- Group information related to one subtopic in one section.

- To build knowledge, Marcus has gathered relevant information from print and digital sources for each of his subtopics.

- He summarizes and explains the information he researched.

SUBTOPIC 2

Underline a sentence that states Marcus's second subtopic.

Circle one piece of information that is relevant to Marcus's analysis of this subtopic.

SUBTOPIC 3

Underline a sentence that states Marcus's third subtopic.

Put a box around the information that Marcus uses to explain this subtopic.

Depending on orbits, Mars is anywhere from 54.6 to 401 million kilometers away from Earth. No one has ever walked on Mars, and no spacecraft has ever traveled back to Earth from Mars. Yet, we have learned much about Mars from rovers. <u>Curiosity</u>, especially, has helped NASA gain valuable information about the possibility that life once existed on Mars. It has also gained data about the planet's atmosphere and geology. Rovers are helping scientists to determine whether humans could be sent to Mars. NASA scientists still have many questions, though. They are still very curious about what life forms might have existed on Mars. <u>Curiosity</u> will likely make many more discoveries that help satisfy NASA's quest for knowledge.

CONCLUDING STATEMENT

Marcus's conclusion wraps up his research on the topic and makes a prediction based on evidence he has presented.

Underline the sentence that states the conclusion most clearly.

Sources:

"Mars Exploration Rovers." <u>NASA.gov</u>. 1 May 2013. http://marsrover.nasa.gov/overview/

Wall, Mike. "Mars Rover Curiosity's 7 Biggest Discoveries (So Far)." <u>Space.com</u>. 1 May 2013. http://www.space.com/20396-mars-rover-curiosity-big-discoveries.html

LIST OF SOURCES

At the end of his report, Marcus provides a list of the digital sources he used for his research.

Use index cards like the ones below to take notes for your research report on a scientific quest. You may use print or digital sources to find information. You will use these notes to create your outline on page 222.

Source 1:

Summarize or paraphrase information:

Source 2:

Summarize or paraphrase information:

Use an outline to organize your research report about a real-life quest. Then write a first draft of your report on a separate sheet of paper. You should have gathered relevant information from print and digital sources and made notes beforehand. You will use this draft to write your final research report in the Unit 10 Review section on page 228.

Title: _____

I. **Introduction**

    a. Topic: _____

    b. Background: _____

    _____

    _____

II. **Subtopic 1:** _____

    a. Fact: _____

    b. Fact: _____

III. **Subtopic 2:** _____

    a. Fact: _____

    b. Fact: _____

IV. **Subtopic 3:** _____

    a. Fact: _____

    b. Fact: _____

V. **Conclusion**

    _____

    _____

    _____

    _____

Commas in Compound Sentences

Guided Instruction A **compound sentence** consists of two independent clauses joined by a conjunction (*and, but, or, for, nor, so, yet*). The **comma** in a compound sentence is always placed before the conjunction.

- INCORRECT
*Ben put the dishes away **and**, he swept the floor.*

- CORRECT
*Ben put the dishes away, **and** he swept the floor.*

Guided Practice Complete each sentence using the conjunction given at the end of the sentence. Add a comma in the correct place.

1. We have math homework _____ we have a spelling worksheet. (and)

2. Kayla can play shortstop _____ she can pitch. (or)

3. Max likes the ocean _____ he does not like lakes. (but)

4. The cars made a lot of noise _____ we shut the window. (so)

Independent Practice Write three of your own compound sentences using the conjunction given. Be sure to place the comma correctly.

1. and

_____

_____

2. or

_____

_____

3. so

_____

_____

Capitalization

Guided Instruction Always begin a sentence with a **capital letter**. Capitalize the first letter of titles, names, proper nouns, and quotations as well.

- *Everyone is excited about the field trip to the Ancient Arts Museum.*

- *Ms. Batra teaches at Central Middle School.*

- *Our teacher said, "Line up for recess."*

Guided Practice Correct the capitalization errors in each sentence.

1. anne and margot, characters in the play <u>the diary of anne frank</u>, are sisters.

_____

_____

2. dr. hugh samuels works at springfield hospital on overton avenue.

_____

3. coach walton shouted to the receiver, "run to the end zone!" as the fans in heinz stadium rose to their feet.

_____

_____

Independent Practice Write three of your own sentences using correct capitalization. Include proper nouns in each sentence. At least one sentence should include a title, and one sentence should include a quotation.

1. _____

_____

2. _____

_____

3. _____

_____

Spelling

Guided Instruction A number of words in the English language may be misspelled quite often. Pay extra attention to these words, and spell them correctly when you write. When you are unsure of how to spell a word, look it up in a dictionary.

Frequently Misspelled Words		
business	familiar	opposite
committee	favorite	particular
disease	interrupt	realize
especially	lightning	scissors
experience	necessary	strengthen

Guided Practice Circle the correct spelling of the word in parentheses.

1. The rainstorm brought thunder and (lightening, lightning).

2. It is (neccesarry, necessary) to take cover during bad weather.

3. The (committee, comittee) will make the decision.

4. What is your (faverit, favorite) book?

5. She set up her (bizness, business) in the new office building.

Independent Practice Find each misspelled word and spell it correctly on the line.

1. Did you relize that you were late?

_____

2. Never run when you are carrying sizzers.

_____

3. He is espeshully tired today.

_____

4. It is rude to inturupt when someone else is talking.

_____

Discuss the Essential Question

How can I develop a topic into a research report?

Think about the Essential Question by responding to the questions below.
Support your point of view with reasons and facts.

1. How does the exploration of Mars with the rover qualify as a quest?

_____

_____

2. What relevant information did the writer include in the report?

_____

_____

Use your notes above to discuss the Essential Question in small groups or as a
class. Follow agreed-upon rules for discussion. Use the organizer below to
record what you heard and how you participated.

Ideas I Agree or Disagree With		Questions I Asked
Agree		
Disagree		
New Ideas I Had During Discussion		**Questions I Answered**

This paragraph has mistakes in comma usage, capitalization, and spelling. Write the paragraph correctly on the lines below.

My favrite book, <u>shipwreck at the bottom of the world</u> by jennifer armstrong, is about ernest shackleton. He was a famous explorer of antarctica. shackleton was not the first person too reach the south pole but, he and his team were the first to climb Mount erebus on Antarctica. In 1911, Shackleton's ship, the <u>endurance</u>, got stuck in the ice and sank. not a single member of it's crew died. Shackleton later wrote a book about there experiance and, he became even more famous.

_____

_____

_____

_____

_____

_____

_____

_____

_____

_____

_____

Assignment: Write a research report about a real-life quest.

On the lines below, write the final copy of the research report draft you created on page 222. Be sure to tell what real-life quest you are writing about and to identify the different aspects of the topic you are covering. Group related information together, and provide a list of sources. See the Writing Handbook (pages 275–283) for ways to improve your writing as you revise.

_____

_____

_____

_____

_____

_____

_____

_____

_____

_____

_____

_____

_____

_____

_____

_____

_____

_____

_____

Introducing UNIT 11

I n this unit about amazing discoveries, you will learn
how knowledge and ideas work together, or integrate,
in informational texts. Authors of informational texts
often include visuals, such as charts, diagrams, graphs, and
time lines. These visual elements are important tools that
can help you more easily visualize and understand
technical and scientific topics.

Authors of informational texts must also give reasons and evidence to
support the points they make. In technical texts, reasons and evidence
often take the form of data. *Data* are facts that can be proven through
observation and measurement. It is your job as a reader to determine
whether the reasons and evidence that an author provides are strong
enough to support the points that he or she is making.

In this unit, you also will learn how to interpret information from two
texts on the same topic, putting information together in order to gain
greater knowledge of the subject. You also will learn how Greek and
Latin roots can help you understand the meanings of words used in
scientific and technical texts.

Before Unit 11 **Progress Check** *Can I?* **After Unit 11**

☐ ☐ Interpret visual information and explain how it helps me
understand a text.

☐ ☐ Explain how an author uses reasons and evidence to support
his or her ideas.

☐ ☐ Gather and put together information by reading two texts on
the same topic.

☐ ☐ Use Greek and Latin roots to help me understand the
meaning of words.

Unit 11 ■ Reading Informational Text: Integration of Knowledge and Ideas **229**

HOME◆CONNECT...

IN THIS UNIT, YOUR CHILD WILL...

- Interpret visual information and other text features in a technical or scientific text.

- Analyze and explain how an author uses reasons and evidence to support his or her ideas.

- Integrate what he or she learns about a subject from two texts and then speak knowledgeably about the information.

- Use common Greek and Latin roots to help define unfamiliar words.

- Compare and contrast four texts on the same theme: a technical text with illustrations, a technical text with diagrams, a paired blog and Internet advertisement, and a paired scientific journal entry and newspaper article.

Nonfiction texts often include **illustrations and other text features**, such as subheadings, captions, and graphs. Ask your child to point out examples in his or her textbooks and to explain how each example makes the text easier to understand.

Authors of nonfiction texts provide **reasons and evidence** to support their ideas. With your child, select an interesting nonfiction text from a book, magazine, newspaper, or website. Read it together and call attention to the reasons and evidence that support the author's main points. Discuss with your child which reasons and evidence are strongest and weakest.

When your child reads a variety of texts on a topic he or she enjoys, he or she can **integrate information**, or put the facts from different texts together, to speak knowledgeably about the topic. Ask your child to share with you what he or she has been learning recently by reading various accounts of a favorite topic.

WAYS TO HELP YOUR CHILD

Encourage your child's growing ability to speak knowledgeably about topics he or she enjoys. Share information about your favorite topics, as well. Talk about the ways you learn new information about your favorite topics. Encourage your child to read about topics that interest him or her and to teach you what he or she learns.

Activity: With your child, use the Internet to search for reliable texts about an amazing discovery or other scientific topic of interest. Print two articles about the topic and read them aloud together. Look for text features, such as diagrams, headings, and captions. Discuss the reasons and evidence the author uses. Talk about information the texts have in common. Then ask your child to tell you about the subject in his or her own words, integrating what he or she has learned.

ONLINE

For more Home Connect activities, continue online at sadlierconnect.com

Reading Informational Text:
Integration of Knowledge and Ideas

Essential Question:
What methods can authors use to present informational texts?

Interpreting Visual Information 232

Analyzing Reasons and Evidence 238

Integrating Information from Texts 244

Close Reading 250

Connect Across Texts 255

Language: Roots. 256

Unit 11 Review .257

WORDS TO KNOW

data

equipped

satellite

Informational text often presents **visual information** in diagrams, charts, photos, and time lines that must be **interpreted**.

CITE EVIDENCE

A To **interpret visual information,** you need to understand how the information is being presented. The time line shows satellites launched between 1957 and 2000, with years listed in ten-year spans. A line leads from each satellite to the time of its launch. Circle the part of the time line that shows when *Explorer I* was launched. What year is this?

B Visuals may restate ideas in the text. In the text, underline the year *Sputnik I* was launched. Put a star at that date on the time line. How does the time line visually reinforce the idea that *Explorer I* was a response to *Sputnik I*?

Satellites Around Earth

(Genre: Technical Text)

1   Look up at the stars on a clear night. If you see a speck of light moving across the sky, you are not looking at a star. Chances are that you are looking at a **satellite**. A satellite is anything that orbits our planet. The moon is a natural satellite. But high above Earth, thousands of satellites made and launched by people are orbiting at this very moment.

2   Satellites serve many purposes. Mostly, they collect scientific **data**. They can gather information on the weather or on big changes in the environment. Some of them even carry large telescopes that can see galaxies many light-years away.

The History of Satellites

3   In the 1950s, the Soviet Union (a group of countries that arose from the former Russian Empire) sent an artificial satellite called *Sputnik I* into space. It went into orbit on October 4, 1957. The United States soon began a "space race" with the Soviet Union by launching a satellite of its own, called *Explorer I*.

4   Both of these early satellites were small metal globes **equipped** with batteries, thermometers, and antennae. They were designed to record scientific data, such as radio waves. *Sputnik* and *Explorer* created an interest in—and a need for—satellite technology that has only increased in the decades since then.

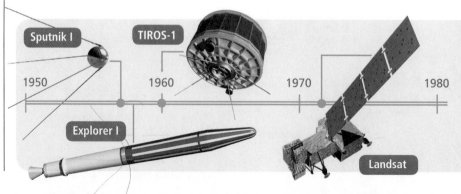

5   After *Explorer I*, the United States launched *TIROS-1*, the first satellite that gathered information about weather. Then came three *Landsat* (short for "land satellite") satellites, the first of which was launched in 1972. These satellites were designed to study how our world changes. Much of what we know about climate change and urban growth comes from *Landsat* data.

6   The launch of the Hubble Space Telescope in 1990 was a major scientific event. Never before had people been able to see such clear images of distant objects in deep space. The Hubble will continue to orbit Earth until 2015.

7   *Ikonos* is an incredibly powerful imaging satellite. An imaging satellite can record images using different parts of the electromagnetic spectrum that humans cannot see. (Regular photographs use only visible light.) Launched in 1999, *Ikonos* offers high-definition pictures of objects on our planet's surface.

8   Many satellites that orbit Earth today deliver media to consumers instantly. Have you ever listened to satellite radio? Think about an international sporting event, like the Olympics. Images from such events probably were sent to you from a satellite like the *Galaxy 14*.

CITE EVIDENCE

C Visuals can also provide information that is not stated directly in the text. On the time line, put a box around the year *TIROS-1* was launched.

D Visual information helps you better understand a text. Read paragraph 8 and then box the spot on the time line that tells when *Galaxy 14* was launched. What year is this? What does the time line visually suggest about how television has changed since the first satellite was launched in 1957?

Comprehension Check

How does the time line help the reader understand the importance of satellites?

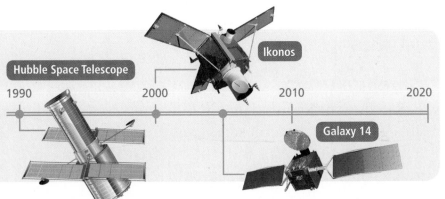

Satellites Around Earth *continued*

Satellites in Space

9   A satellite is usually launched into space on a rocket. When the space shuttle program was active, satellites could also be delivered into orbit by a space shuttle.

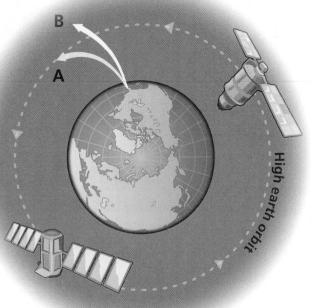

10   The rocket that launches a satellite must be very powerful, for satellites can be quite heavy. Some satellites weigh several tons! The rocket fires special engines called *boosters* to get it off the ground. Once in space, the rocket fires smaller rockets that tip it into place. Then the rocket releases the satellite into a circular orbit around Earth.

11   It is important to balance the speed of Earth's rotation with the satellite's motion. If the satellite moves too slowly, Earth's gravity will pull it down. That would be a disaster, for satellites are costly to produce and launch. Scientists devote many years to the development of just one satellite. What about the danger to people if a satellite falls? Fortunately, most pieces of a satellite would burn up in Earth's atmosphere before landing.

12   An **orbital velocity** is the speed at which a satellite needs to move in order to stay in a steady orbit around Earth. A satellite that is 150 miles above Earth should have an orbital velocity of about 17,000 miles per hour. The satellite must not go too fast, though. If it does, it can reach **escape velocity**. Escape velocity is the speed at which the satellite will break out of its orbit and shoot off into space.

Satellite Orbits

13   Satellites orbit our planet in different ways. A satellite in a geostationary orbit stays over the same spot on Earth at all times. This is the best kind of orbit for satellites that study the weather.

WORDS TO KNOW

escape velocity

orbital velocity

CITE EVIDENCE

A Circle the satellites shown in the diagram above.

B In paragraph 12, underline two terms that correspond to A and B in the diagram. What is the purpose of the diagram?

14   In the case of a polar orbit, a satellite traces a line past the North and South Poles. Earth rotates beneath this imaginary orbit. This kind of orbit is ideal for satellites used for mapping.

Comprehension Check

1. Which of the following terms from the text is NOT illustrated in the diagram on page 234?

   a. orbital velocity

   b. escape velocity

   c. geostationary orbit

   d. satellite

2. Which of the following best explains the meaning of *orbital velocity*?

   a. the speed at which a satellite needs to move in order to stay in a steady orbit around Earth

   b. an orbit in which a satellite stays over the same spot on Earth at all times

   c. an orbit in which a satellite traces a line past the North and South Poles

   d. the speed at which a satellite will break out of its orbit and shoot off into space

3. Work with a partner. Discuss how the diagram on page 234 helps you understand how satellites move in space. Cite details from the text in your answer.

   A satellite in a geostationary orbit stays over the same sport on Earth at all times.

Independent Practice

Satellites Around Earth *continued*

WORDS TO KNOW

calculate

innovative

range

CITE EVIDENCE

A The diagram on this page shows how GPS fleet technology works. Find and underline the text that corresponds to Step 3 in the diagram.

B In the GPS fleet diagram, put a box around the GPS satellites. How would a car with a built-in GPS differ from what the diagram shows?

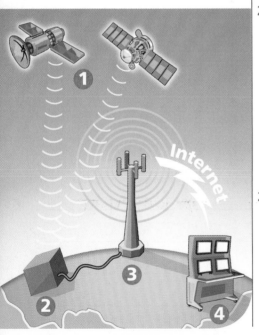

How Far Above Earth?

15   As you have learned, satellites orbit many miles above Earth's surface. But there is a wide **range** in the height of these orbits.

16   The satellites that are closest orbit 80–1,200 miles above the surface. The *Landsat* satellites that do mapping are examples of relatively close satellites.

17   Farther away are scientific satellites that gather data on the environment. They orbit 3,000–6,000 miles above the surface. Next are satellites that help with navigation, such as GPS satellites. They are 6,000–12,000 miles away.

18   Farthest away, at more than 22,000 miles, are satellites that tell us about the weather and that help with communication, such as television and radio satellites.

GPS Satellites

19   Among the most **innovative** satellites are the GPS (Global Positioning System) satellites. The U.S. government originally designed them for military use. GPS technology is now used by many people to help with mapping locations.

20   GPS technology starts with a series of 24–32 satellites. These satellites communicate with devices on the ground called GPS receivers. The receivers exchange radio signals with at least three GPS satellites. First, the receivers **calculate** how long it takes the signals to reach the satellites. Then they measure their distance to the satellites. The receivers collect this data and use it to determine an exact location.

21   Today, GPS receivers are built into cars and smartphones. Some companies use GPS to track an entire fleet of vehicles. In this case, the GPS receivers' location data is sent to a cellular phone network. The network then sends the information, via the Internet, to computers.

22   The computers that receive this information have software that can assemble the location data. For example, a police department might have a special bank of computers using GPS to track its police cars. A trucking company might use GPS to locate its trucks as they deliver shipments.

23   GPS technology is just one of the many ways that artificial satellites are being used to make life better in today's world.

Comprehension Check

(MORE ONLINE) **sadlierconnect.com**

1. Which of the following does Step 2 in the diagram on page 236 represent?

(a.) the Internet

b. GPS satellites

c. a GPS receiver

d. a bank of computers

2. Suppose that the diagram showed a smartphone with a built-in GPS. Where in the diagram would the smartphone appear?

a. Step 1

b. Step 2

c. Step 3

(d.) Step 4

3. How does the diagram on page 236 help the reader understand the text description of how GPS fleet technology works?

I works they have to receivers are built into cars and smartphones.

WORDS TO KNOW

converted

electromagnetic spectrum

neutralize

refracted

An author uses **reasons and evidence** to support the particular points he or she makes in a text.

CITE EVIDENCE

A **Evidence** for ideas can appear as words or as images. For example, in paragraph 2, the idea that there are different kinds of energy waves is supported by the diagram. Put a star by the section of the diagram that shows the range of visible light.

B In paragraph 3, underline the names of the four devices that are used as evidence to support the idea that machines have been built to use the invisible waves in the electromagnetic spectrum. How are these machines useful to people? What would change if they had never been invented?

Becoming Invisible:
Fantasy or Fact?
(Genre: Technical Text)

1   Have you ever imagined what it would be like to become invisible? It's just a fantasy, right? Actually, invisibility is not totally impossible; in fact, scientists are conducting experiments today to see how to make people, objects, and even buildings and vehicles invisible!

How We See

2   The science of invisibility begins with understanding how we see. When we look at something, we are not seeing the actual object. Instead, we are seeing the light that reflects off of the object. Light is a kind of energy that is made up of waves. There are many different kinds of waves that make up the **electromagnetic spectrum**. Although the human eye can see only the waves that are in the "visible light" range of the spectrum, certain animals can see, or sense, other parts of the electromagnetic spectrum. Rattlesnakes, for example, can "see" infrared light, and bees can sense ultraviolet light.

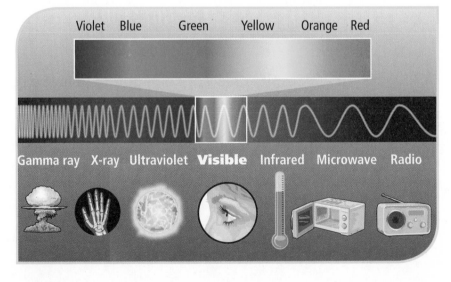

3   People have invented machines to use the waves on the spectrum that we cannot see. A microwave oven uses microwaves to heat food. X-ray machines are used to photograph a person's bones. Radio waves are **converted** into sound—music or voices—by a radio. Cell phone signals are also on the spectrum.

4   Electromagnetic waves have many interesting properties. For example, visible light can be reflected, or thrown back, from something. You can see reflection in action when you point a flashlight at a mirror. Light also can be **refracted**, or bent. Perhaps you've seen an example of refraction when you shone a light through a prism or crystal and a little rainbow appeared. In outer space, light bends when it goes past a planet. This bending occurs because the planet's gravity bends the light.

Invisibility

5   Scientists have wondered for a long time about electromagnetic waves and their properties. If we see light waves because the waves bounce off objects, then perhaps there is a way to **neutralize** the waves, or cancel them out.

6   What if a material could refract the waves around, or away from, an object? Then the object couldn't be seen. In a sense, it would be "hidden." A Russian scientist first thought of this idea in the 1960s, but that idea has led today to a breakthrough in invisibility: metamaterials.

Comprehension Check

Why does the author tell about the properties of electromagnetic waves before discussing invisibility?

CITE EVIDENCE

C In paragraph 4, circle a sentence that gives evidence for the idea that light can be reflected.

D Reread paragraph 5. Underline the scientific reasoning behind the idea that electromagnetic waves might be neutralized. How does that idea relate to invisibility?

ANALYZING REASONS AND EVIDENCE

Becoming Invisible: Fantasy or Fact? *continued*

Metamaterials

WORDS TO KNOW

distort

interact

manipulate

CITE EVIDENCE

A In paragraph 7, circle the sentence that supports the information in the diagram on page 241.

B In paragraph 11, underline the two sentences that give evidence for the idea that exciting advances in metamaterial technology are being made in this early part of the twenty-first century. What might be some of the results of these advances?

7   Metamaterials are at the cutting edge of invisibility technology. What are metamaterials? They are materials that have been designed with unusual qualities, or properties—properties that no natural object could have. (*Meta* means "going beyond.") Metamaterials were inspired by the idea that electromagnetic waves can be refracted, or redirected, around an object.

8   Metamaterials are extremely small. They are made of microscopically small elements, in fact, since they have to be smaller than the size of the electromagnetic wave that is racing toward them.

9   How do metamaterials work? When a wave hits a normal object, it **interacts** with the object's structure. That is why the object can be seen or sensed. Engineers have changed the structures of metamaterials so that the waves will behave differently when they hit the material. The structure of a metamaterial **distorts** the waves and sends them around the object. As a result, the object cannot be sensed.

10   An experiment done in 2006 showed that a fabric-like metamaterial, a kind of thin cloak, could refract microwaves. The "fabric" was made of very tiny rings. But microwaves, which are not visible to the human eye, are longer waves than visible light. A metamaterial that could refract the shorter waves of visible light would have to be composed of even smaller materials.

11   Just about a year later, though, there were several advances in metamaterials technology. In 2007, a scientist developed a metamaterial that could refract visible light. The only problem was that the material was extremely small. It was just 10 micrometers thick, or thinner than a human hair! That same year, some Chinese physicists developed metamaterials that could **manipulate** a different kind of wave: sound waves.

12   Metamaterial technology is still in its earliest days, but its future looks bright. Scientists are still looking into ways to create metamaterials that can act as "cloaking devices" to make people, vehicles, and even buildings invisible. But metamaterials are not the only path to invisibility.

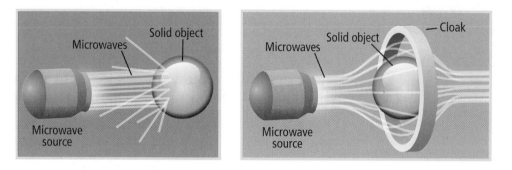

Comprehension Check

1. What evidence supports the point that metamaterials are not natural materials?

   a. Some metamaterials are made of tiny rings.

   b. Metamaterials are extremely small.

   (c.) Metamaterials can do things that natural materials cannot do.

   d. Metamaterials can reflect and refract light.

2. To create "invisibility," metamaterials must have a changed structure. What reason does the author give to support this point?

   (a.) Electromagnetic waves interact with most structures.

   b. Some metamaterials are able to manipulate sound waves.

   c. Metamaterials are extremely small.

   d. Electromagnetic waves cannot be refracted.

3. What reasons does the author give to support the idea that the future of metamaterials looks bright?

   Metamaterials help you build things and help you with science

Becoming Invisible: Fantasy or Fact? *continued*

Optical Camouflage

13   Another technology can create a kind of "invisibility": optical **camouflage**. When you see the word *camouflage*, you might think of the patterned uniforms that soldiers or hunters wear to blend in outdoors, or the way chameleons change color to match their surroundings. Optical camouflage is not quite so simple.

14   The first thing you will need for optical camouflage is a special item of clothing—a cloak—that is covered in very small beads. These beads have been engineered to refract light in a precise way so that the light bounces back in the same direction that it came from. This process is called **retro-reflection**. Retro-reflection exists in everyday life; for example, bicycle reflectors are retro-reflective and can be seen by nighttime drivers.

15   Your cloak is just the beginning. You will need some other equipment. First, set up a digital video camera so that it is at your back, pointed away from you. Record video footage of what is happening behind you.

16   Then you will need a computer that will process the images you recorded. You also will need a **projector** that can display the images on your special retro-reflective cloak. The film must be projected through a very small hole so that the images in the film match up with the size of your cloak.

17   You will need one more thing: a special mirror. This mirror will reflect the film onto the cloak and will send the film images back to the viewer. The mirror also will direct other surrounding light to the viewer. The mirror is important for the final effect: Viewers should be able to see the environment as well as the person who is wearing the cloak.

18   The final effect will be similar to what happens when you walk in front of a movie screen while a movie is being projected: You take on the appearance of your

WORDS TO KNOW

camouflage

projector

retro-reflection

CITE EVIDENCE

A In paragraph 14, put a star by a sentence that supports the idea that retro-reflection is commonly used.

B In paragraph 16, underline the reason that the film must be projected through a small hole. How difficult does this process seem?

background. But the background will blend into the image on your cloak, and you won't cast a black shadow behind you. With optical camouflage, you won't be completely invisible, but you won't be immediately noticeable, either.

19   Some invisibility is possible today, but only through complex and expensive technologies like metamaterials and optical camouflage. In the future, there will likely be simpler, more accessible ways to become fully invisible. Invisibility will no longer be a fantasy, but a reality.

Comprehension Check

MORE ONLINE   sadlierconnect.com

1. Which piece of equipment is NOT needed for optical camouflage?

   a. a special mirror

   b. a projector

   c. a digital video camera

   d. a cloak made of metamaterials

2. Which statement best explains the purpose of the special mirror in optical camouflage?

   a. It refracts light in the exact same direction that it came from.

   b. The viewer looks at the final image in it.

   c. It reflects the film onto a special cloak.

   d. It projects the image onto a special movie screen.

3. What evidence in this section supports the author's point that invisibility is a complex and expensive technology? Cite evidence in your answer.

   That cloaks are invisibil and it reflects the film.

Guided Instruction

WORDS TO KNOW

fossil fuel
nonrenewable resource
renewable resource
sustainable

> If you read more than one text about a topic, you can **integrate the information,** or combine it, in order to write or speak more knowledgeably about the topic.

CITE EVIDENCE

A You will be reading two texts about energy consumption and then **integrating the information** from both. In this first text, a blog, the author names problems with consuming too much energy. In paragraph 2, put a star by one of those problems.

B In paragraph 3, underline the example that supports the idea that people are overusing Earth's natural resources. Why is this a problem?

Let's Go Green!

by Vera S. Roshinski, MS in Environmental Science

(Genre: Blog)

1   As regular readers of my blog know, I'm a big fan of green energy. This rapidly growing area of science and technology develops environmentally friendly and self-sustaining energy sources.

2   Why green energy? Consider this: The developed nations are consuming too much energy. This overuse puts a terrible strain on Earth's natural resources. People can do many things to reduce their consumption of natural resources. I want to share some ideas. But first, let's be clear about how much energy we are using and why it's a problem.

Reducing Energy Consumption

3   There are many ways to measure our overuse of natural resources. Perhaps the most striking is our dependence on **fossil fuels.** Fossil fuels are resources that come from the earth. Oil, coal, and natural gas are fossil fuels that we use to generate electricity.

4   Fossil fuels are **nonrenewable resources**. In other words, someday they will be completely used up. Switching to **renewable resources** will keep us from depending on fossil fuels for all of our energy needs. These **sustainable** sources of energy—"green" energy— include wind power, solar power, and geothermal power.

5   Oil is an example of fossil fuel consumption. Most kinds of transportation require the use of oil. Oil also heats homes and businesses. Right now, the United States ranks first in the world in oil consumption. In fact, Americans use about 22% of all the oil in the world each year. But other large nations, such as China and India, are becoming big consumers of oil, too.

6   As we use up oil, its price rises. The price of oil has risen dramatically in recent decades, putting a strain on American families' budgets.

Protecting the Environment

7   Using fossil fuels can also harm the environment. Just obtaining the resources can be damaging. Both drilling for oil and mining for coal can harm the natural habitats of plants and animals living nearby.

8   Additionally, when the resources are used, they cause pollution. Burning coal, for example, releases carbon dioxide into the air. Many scientists link the increase in carbon dioxide to global warming, which has caused its own environmental problems. In addition, pollutants in the air harm humans, animals, and plants.

CITE EVIDENCE

C As you read information, you want to remember it so that you can **speak or write on the subject knowledgeably** and with confidence. In paragraph 5, circle the specific information about how much oil the United States consumes.

D In paragraph 8, underline information about how using fossil fuels damages the environment. How does this information relate to the topic of green energy?

Comprehension Check

Summarize in your own words the two main reasons that the blogger is arguing in favor of using green energy sources.

Guided Practice

Let's Go Green! *continued*

Green Architecture

WORDS TO KNOW

conservation

principle

CITE EVIDENCE

A In paragraphs 10 and 11, put boxes around three ways that the California Academy of Sciences building is saving on energy costs.

B Review the section "Going Green at Home." Underline four ways that people can save energy at home. Then discuss which of the suggestions you and your family already do.

9   The ideal way for a business to "go green" is to follow the **principles** of green architecture in its building construction. Green architecture requires that people think about energy **conservation** and environmental protection before a building is built.

10   The California Academy of Sciences building in San Francisco is an award-winning green building. Its "Living Roof" is covered with six inches of soil that not only grows native plants but also provides insulation, saves rainwater, and helps to direct air currents. Skylights in the roof save on heating and cooling costs by releasing hot air from inside and bringing in cool air from outside. Solar panels on the roof are a sustainable energy feature that provides electricity.

11   Special glass was used to create the transparent outer walls. These glass walls bring in natural light, thus cutting down on electricity costs.

12   The building also runs on the principle that "warm air rises." Instead of using a forced-air central heating system that would waste energy in such a large space with high ceilings, hot water running through tubes under the floors provides heat that rises. And recycled denim jeans are used to insulate the building!

Going Green at Home

13   You don't have to be a big business or organization to go green. You can do a lot at home.

14   If you need to purchase appliances, such as washers and dryers, look for an EnergyGuide label. The label tells you that the U.S. Department of Energy has approved the appliance to be energy efficient.

15   Set air conditioners on timers so that they are not running all the time, especially when no one is home.

16   Recycle materials. Use old T-shirts to wash the car. Save glass jars for leftovers. You'll reduce the energy needed to make new products.

17   Start a carpool to save gas. Ask your parents to take you and your friends to school all in one car. Or take the bus!

18   If businesses and people go green together, everyone will conserve energy and protect the environment.

> Comments . . .

Post

Comprehension Check

1. One way in which the California Academy of Sciences has saved energy is by

   a. never heating the building at all.

   b. using a lot of glass in the building's construction.

   c. dumping rainwater as quickly as possible.

   d. using skylights on the roof to save on heating and cooling costs.

2. Why does the author suggest recycling materials in your home?

   a. Recycling is easier than shopping for new products.

   b. Recycling will lead to fewer new products being produced.

   c. Recycling is approved by the U.S. Department of Energy.

   d. Recycling is the easiest way to "go green."

3. How are the ways that businesses and people can "go green" similar and different? Discuss this question with a partner. Be sure to cite evidence from the text.

_____

_____

_____

_____

WORDS TO KNOW

compatible

emit

fixture

CITE EVIDENCE

A Put a box around the text in the ad that would be a good fit in the blogger's list of "Going Green at Home" ideas.

B Underline information in the ad that tells about the energy efficiency of LED light bulbs. What do you think the blogger would say about the way that LED light bulbs impact the environment?

LED Lights

(Genre: Internet Advertisement)

http://www.trulybetterLEDbulbs.com

Choose LED light bulbs

for your home or office!

If you care about saving energy, saving the environment, AND saving money . . .

LED stands for "light-emitting diode."
LED light bulbs **emit** light from a solid, not a gas or a vacuum!

WHY choose LED light bulbs?

- They're as much as 85% more energy efficient than regular light bulbs!
- Regular light bulbs lose up to 80% of their energy in heat. LED light bulbs lose less than 20%!
- They're cool—literally! You can unscrew an LED light bulb while it's still on—it won't be hot!
- They aren't a fire hazard, like regular light bulbs!
- LED light bulbs release less carbon dioxide into the atmosphere—much better for the environment!
- You can get up to 100,000 hours of light from a single bulb, compared to about 750 hours from a traditional bulb!
- They're **compatible** with all **fixture** types!
- You get up to 60 watts of light using only 7.5 watts of power!
- You'll love their SOFT WHITE light!

Check out our website for pricing information... you won't believe the MONEY YOU'LL SAVE in the long run! www.trulybetterLEDbulbs.com

Truly Better LED Bulbs, Inc.

1. Where would the blogger in the first selection be most likely to put information about LED lights?

   a. in the section "Going Green at Home"

   b. in her description of how fossil fuels harm the environment

   c. in her description of the California Academy of Sciences building

   d. as a main part of her argument about the need for green energy

2. Which of the following statements in this ad about how LED light bulbs are different from traditional light bulbs would NOT be information that the blogger would use to support the use of LED lights?

   a. LED light bulbs are better for the environment.

   b. LED light bulbs last much longer than regular light bulbs.

   c. LED light bulbs emit light from a solid, not a gas or a vacuum.

   d. LED light bulbs are more energy efficient.

3. Think about the information in the blog and in the advertisement for the light bulbs. In what ways are LED light bulbs a form of green energy that the blogger would approve of? Cite evidence from both texts to support your answer.

   _____

   _____

   _____

   _____

   _____

   _____

   _____

   _____

The Robot Cheetah

(Genre: Scientific Journal Entry)

1   I have been working on a special robotics program for several years, but I haven't written about it before now. It's been in early experimental stages for a long time. But since we've now had some success, it's time to write about the story.

2   I've been part of a scientific team that has developed a robot that can run faster than a human being! And here is the coolest thing: The robot is a cheetah!

Imitating Nature

3   I should begin by giving some background information about an exciting field of science that has a lot of impact on robotics. It is called biomimetics.

4   Biomimetics is a field of science that looks to nature for ideas. For example, in the earliest days of airplanes, people studied birds to learn principles that they could apply to flying machines. So, biomimetics is basically a way of imitating, or mimicking, nature.

5   Biomimetics urges humans to look to nature for ideas of how to do things more efficiently. In nature, there are many examples of energy efficiency— including the way some animals move.

6   Biomimetics is often used to help solve problems. What problem does our cheetah solve?

7   The robot cheetah has been part of a series of inventions funded by the United States Defense Department, which is responsible for the nation's security and armed forces.

8 For years, some people have dreamed of developing a robot that could replace a soldier. Soldiers can be killed or wounded, but a robot cannot. Nor can a robot get sick or tired.

9 Since many animals are stronger and more agile than humans, people started to imagine robotic animals that could be sent into hostile places. Such robots could deliver equipment, rescue humans, or even do the fighting in dangerous areas.

Studying the Cheetah

10 The cheetah was a perfect animal to study. It is a very strong, fast creature.

11 We focused on the cheetah's legs and its enormously long and powerful running strides. We designed special motors that imitated the movements of the cheetah's legs and shoulders.

12 We built a mechanical metal body to house these motors, and everything had to be connected. It took a long time, but we finally got our cheetah robot ready for a test run. We put it on a treadmill and began our test.

13 I should mention that in the early days, we got the robot cheetah to *trot* rather than *run*. Still, it could trot at a pace of 5 miles per hour for 90 minutes before slowing down.

14 A few months ago, our four-legged cheetah robot got up to 18 miles per hour. During our most recent test, our robot ran 28.3 miles per hour! That's even faster than the fastest human, who can run at an average speed of 23 miles per hour! Real cheetahs can run up to—and sometimes even faster than—60 miles per hour. That speed is our ultimate goal.

Robot Cheetah			Fastest Human	Real Cheetah
First Run	Second Run	Third Run		
5 mph	18 mph	28.3 mph	23 mph	60+ mph

Run, Robot, Run

15   So far, we have had to hold the cheetah robot in place with overhead cords. The robot is powered by hydraulics. In hydraulics, a fluid is pumped into a machine through a hose. Pressure builds and makes the machine move.

16   The robot cheetah has very high energy efficiency, even with the use of hydraulics. We're still trying to improve its efficiency, though. Robots use a lot of energy, and they often have to carry a heavy power source. Even then, their power doesn't last very long. We really have to "think green" when we're working on robotic energy efficiency.

17   We need to give our cheetah more power so it will run faster. We want it to run without having cords connected to it. Our goal is a faster robot cheetah that can run freely outdoors. We built something close to it a few years ago.

The BigDog

18   Our BigDog, as we called it, was a robot animal on four legs that could run outside without any cords attached. We tested it on snow and ice and it still worked. And—this is impressive—it could run for a distance of 20 miles with 400 pounds strapped to its back! Now you get a sense of the potential of these robot animals.

Into the Future

19   We're hoping that sometime in the next year or two we'll have a freer, more powerful version of our robot cheetah to reveal to the world. Imagine if we can get it to run at speeds of 60 miles an hour! It will be a huge break-through in the field of robotics. When it happens, I'll write about it, too!

Robot Cheetah on the Move

by Paula Z. Kay, Science Reporter

(Genre: Newspaper Article)

20 Last week, a local advanced robotics laboratory revealed that it had developed a robot cheetah that could run faster than the world's fastest human being.

21 This same laboratory had designed a so-called BigDog a few years ago, and it was a sight to behold: a computerized metal beast with four legs, hauling hundreds of pounds.

22 But the BigDog ran only 4 miles per hour. This robot cheetah has already run more than 28 miles per hour.

23 The robot cheetah is an odd-looking beast. It's all metal parts, wires, and cords. And it has no skin, so it is hard to recognize as a cheetah.

24 However, its movements are based on a real cheetah's movements. When it starts to move, it is an amazing thing. First comes the clicking of its metal feet on the treadmill. The pace of the clicking increases, and soon the whole thing is clicking, shaking, and then actually running.

25 Their next version of the cheetah, which will be called the WildCat, will run outdoors—and even faster.

Comprehension Check

1. What reason does the author of the journal give to support the idea that the robot cheetah is connected to the world of green energy?

   a. The robot runs on natural gas.

   b. The robot has a very high energy efficiency.

   c. The robot can run faster than a human being.

   d. The robot can haul hundreds of pounds.

2. Which of the following facts about the robot cheetah is found only in the short newspaper article?

   a. It can run faster than a human being.

   b. It is made of metal.

   c. It is powered by hydraulics and is held up by an overhanging cord.

   d. The next version of the robot cheetah will be named WildCat.

3. In the scientific journal entry, how does the information presented in the chart help the reader better understand the topic?

_____

_____

_____

_____

_____

_____

_____

_____

4. How is the robot cheetah an example of biomimetics? Cite evidence from the journal to support your answer.

_____

_____

_____

_____

_____

_____

_____

_____

Compare and Contrast Texts

In this unit, you read texts about amazing scientific and technological discoveries. Think about what you learned from these texts. Then choose two of the texts and compare and contrast them using the T-chart below. List key details and important points from the texts to show the similarities and differences between them. Be prepared to discuss your ideas with your class.

Similarities	Differences

Return to the Essential Question

What methods can authors use to present informational texts?

In small groups or as a class, discuss the Essential Question. Think about what you have learned from integrating texts about the same topic and from looking at the evidence and reasoning that an author provides. Also think about how information that was presented visually supported the main text. Use evidence from the unit texts to answer the question.

Roots

Guided Instruction If you read a word that is unfamiliar to you, check if it has a familiar Greek or Latin root. That root can provide you with a clue to the word's meaning.

The root of a word is the middle part, often unrecognizable, without any prefix or suffix attached to it. For example, the Latin root *ben-* means "good" or "well." A *benefit*, then, is a good or helpful result.

This chart shows the meaning of some Latin and Greek roots.

Greek or Latin Root	Meaning of Root	Example
-auto-	self	automatic
-bio-	life	biology
-flect-, -flex-	bend	deflect, flexible
-fract-	break	fracture
-geo-	earth	geology
-graph-	draw, write	graphic
-micro-	small	microwave
-phot-	light	photoelectric
-scope-	see, watch	telescope
-therm-	heat	thermal

Guided Practice Underline the root in each of the following words. Then write the meaning of the word on the line.

1. automobile _____

2. reflect _____

3. photograph _____

4. biography _____

Independent Practice Read the following sentences. Find the word that has at least one Greek or Latin root. Then underline the root or roots and write the meaning on the line.

1. You can use a microscope to see single-celled organisms.

_____

2. Renewable sources of "green" energy include wind power, solar power, and geothermal power.

_____

Read the passage and look at the time line. Pay attention to any evidence the author offers to support his or her ideas. Also, look for word roots. Then answer the questions on page 258.

Wind:
Energy for Today and Tomorrow
(Genre: Technical Text)

1 Using the power of the wind has become a popular energy alternative to burning fossil fuels. Wind power is harnessed on wind farms, where wind turbines spin as the wind blows. The turbines convert wind into electricity.

2 Wind power produces thousands of megawatts of electricity all over the world. Currently, wind accounts for about 3.5% of all electricity produced in the United States. There is a plan to generate 20% of the nation's electricity from wind power by the year 2030.

3 Wind energy is a clean kind of energy. It does not require the burning of fossil fuels, so no carbon dioxide is released into the air. Therefore, it does not contribute to global warming. Harnessing wind power also does not pollute water, as coal mining does.

4 Studies show that wind power could provide ten times as much electricity as the country needs. Nations around the world are considering how strong a commitment they will make to this promising energy source.

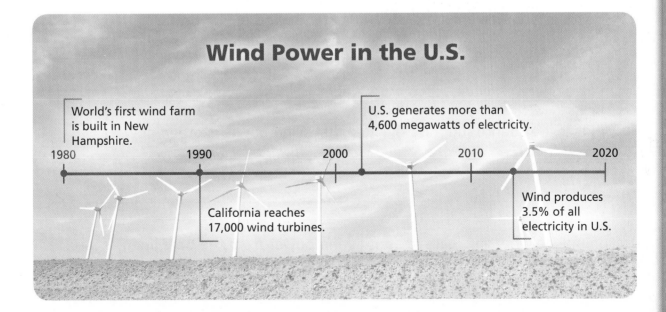

Wind Power in the U.S.

World's first wind farm is built in New Hampshire.

1980   1990   2000   2010   2020

California reaches 17,000 wind turbines.

U.S. generates more than 4,600 megawatts of electricity.

Wind produces 3.5% of all electricity in U.S.

1. Circle the correct choice. According to the time line, the world's first wind farm was built (in California in 1990 / in New Hampshire in 1980).

2. Circle the correct choice. The fact that wind produces 3.5% of the nation's electricity appears (in the text and the time line / in the time line only).

3. The Latin root of the word *popular* is most likely

   ○ *-pop-*, meaning "busy."   ○ *-po-*, meaning "poor."

   ○ *-popu-*, meaning "loud."   ○ *-popul-*, meaning "people."

4. Circle the correct choice. The Greek root *-gen-* means "birth." The word *generate* likely refers to (becoming older / producing something).

5. In the text, underline evidence that the U.S. is committed to wind power.

6. Circle the word in paragraph 3 that has a Latin root meaning "sphere."

7. What else might you need to learn about wind power before you could write or talk confidently about it?

   _____

   _____

8. How does the time line help you understand wind power better?

   _____

   _____

9. What text evidence supports the idea that wind power is green power?

   _____

   _____

10. Summarize what you learned about wind power from the time line.

    _____

    _____

There are three parts to this performance task. Your teacher will provide you with copies of three selections.

- *An Ancient Discovery* Genre: Realistic Fiction
- *Journal of an Archaeologist* Genre: Journal
- *Career Ideas: Archaeologist* Genre: Informational Text

Part 1: Literary Analysis

☐ Read An Ancient Discovery carefully. Take notes that will help you understand the passage.

☐ Answer Items 1–3 on pages 260–261.

☐ Then read the prompt for Item 4 and write two paragraphs on your own paper. You may want to make some notes on scratch paper first.

Part 2: Narrative Writing

☐ Read *Journal of an Archaeologist* carefully. Take notes that will help you understand the passage.

☐ Answer Items 1–2 about *Journal of an Archaeologist* on page 262.

☐ Review *An Ancient Discovery*. You will use both passages in this task.

☐ Then read the prompt for Item 3 and write an essay on your own paper. You may want to make some notes on scratch paper first.

Part 3: Research Simulation

☐ Read *Career Ideas: Archaeologist* carefully. Take notes that will help you understand the passage.

☐ Answer Items 1–3 about *Career Ideas: Archaeologist* on pages 263–264.

☐ Review *Journal of an Archaeologist*. You will use both passages in this task.

☐ Then read the prompt for Item 4 and write an essay on your own paper. You may want to make some notes on scratch paper first.

Part 1 Literary Analysis

Read all parts of the question before responding. Circle the correct answer to Items 1–3. Use your own paper to respond to Item 4.

Item 1

Part A Which three words best describe Rumi in the story *An Ancient Discovery*?

a. gentle and shy

b. lucky and bored

c. curious and helpful

d. strong and hungry

Part B Which details from the story support the answer to Part A?

a. Rumi sees a lot of people at the first dig site. He finds another site that his uncle had shown him.

b. Rumi wants to see the dig site. He carries supplies up the mountainside and helps Jill.

c. Rumi brushes dirt off the pottery. He asks his father questions.

d. Rumi eats breakfast quickly. He spends the day outdoors.

Item 2

Part A What is the main theme of *An Ancient Discovery*?

a. Even someone who is young can volunteer and be helpful.

b. It is important to respect your parents and other adults and to listen to what they say.

c. Pay attention and be careful when you work.

d. If you get bored, use your imagination.

Part B Which details from the story best support the answer to Part A?

   a. Rumi asked to go with his father. He had to stay behind.

   b. Rumi's uncle showed him ancient ruins. The ruins were in the jungle.

   c. Rumi pretended to be an archaeologist. His father worked as a guide.

   d. Rumi helped measure stone walls. He led them to a new dig site.

Item 3

Part A What does the word *geography* mean in this sentence from *An Ancient Discovery*?

His father knew a lot about the local *geography*.

   a. the study of archaeology

   b. the language spoken in an area

   c. the history of a people and their culture

   d. the location of land features such as mountains

Part B Which word part helps the reader understand the meaning of *geography*? What does the word part mean?

   a. *graph* means "to speak"

   b. *geo* means "earth or ground"

   c. *ogra* means "the past"

   d. *graphy* means "to dig"

Item 4

Think about Rumi's actions in the story and the events that took place. How are Rumi's actions and the story events related? Write two paragraphs to explain your answer. Use details from the story to help your answer.

Part 2 Narrative Writing

Read all parts of the question before responding. Circle the correct answer to Items 1–2. Use your own paper to respond to Item 3.

Item 1

Part A What is the overall structure of the text *Journal of an Archaeologist*?

   a. cause and effect

   b. problem and solution

   c. sequence of events

   d. comparison of ideas

Part B What features in the text support the answer to Part A?

   a. The text gives facts about history.

   b. The text tells what happens on each date.

   c. The text explains that archaeology is dirty work.

   d. The text explains what people ate in ancient times.

Item 2

What is the meaning of "unlocks the mysteries of the past" in the text? I get to be a part of a team that unlocks the mysteries of the past...

   a. discovers and shares information about history

   b. writes books about people and places

   c. enjoys stories about Roman people

   d. uncovers buried items in the dirt

Item 3

Think about the events described in *An Ancient Discovery* and *Journal of an Archaeologist*. Write two or three paragraphs explaining how the journal entries would be different if the writer was at a dig site in Peru instead of England. Describe what happens in a series of journal entries told in first person. Use ideas and facts from both passages to support your writing.

Part 3 Research Simulation

Read all parts of the question before responding. Circle the correct answer to Items 1–3. Use your own paper to respond to Item 4.

Item 1

Part A According to *Career Ideas: Archaeologist*, what is one reason you might become an historical archaeologist?

a. because you might be part of a field crew that excavates

b. because you can excavate abandoned ships and airplanes

c. because you want to study relationships between Earth and people

d. because you like to read family records, diaries, letters, and maps

Part B Which sentence from the text supports the answer to Part A?

a. "A little water won't stop an archaeologist!"

b. "Sometimes they find the actual artifacts described."

c. "They look for ecofacts (natural remains)."

d. "They dig everywhere, including in old garbage piles."

Item 2

Part A What is the main idea of *Career Ideas: Archaeologist*?

a. Archaeologists have field crews that excavate.

b. Archaeologists excavate abandoned ships.

c. Archaeologists read historical documents.

d. Archaeologists have interesting jobs.

Part B Which sentence from the text supports the answer to Part A?

a. "If you like to read family records, diaries, letters, and maps..."

b. "Archaeology is tons of mystery-solving fun."

c. "Many archaeology projects have field crews who are new."

d. "Their work tells us about seafaring life and culture."

Item 3

Part A   Which dictionary entry below best defines **degree** as it is used in this sentence from the text?

They might have a **degree** in archaeology.

de·gree (di-ˈgrē)

1. a step or stage in a process

2. the amount of burn damage done to skin by heat

3. a title given to students for completing a program of study

4. a unit of measurement used to tell temperatures

    a. 1   **b.** 2   **c.** 3   **d.** 4

Part B   Which key words in the Part A dictionary entries help the reader know which entry is the correct definition?

a. damage, heat

b. students, study

c. step, process

d. measurement, temperatures

Item 4

You have read two texts describing the job of an archaeologist. Think about the point of view and the facts in *Journal of an Archaeologist* and *Career Ideas: Archaeologist*. How are the two passages alike? How are they different? Write two or three paragraphs that compare and contrast the point of view and information provided in each text.

Foundational Skills Handbook

Base Words 266

Prefixes. 267

Suffixes. 268

Latin and Greek Roots 269

Open and Closed Syllables 270

Syllables with Vowel Teams . . . 271

Syllables with *r*-Controlled
Vowels 272

Words with Silent Consonants . . 273

Practicing Fluency. 274

Base Words

A **base word** is a complete word that makes sense on its own. Many words are formed by adding a prefix or suffix to a base word. Recognizing the base word can help you read and understand these words.

Look at this chart to see how the base word agree is changed by adding prefixes and suffixes.

Word	Prefix	Base Word	Suffix	Meaning
agree**ment**		agree	**ment**	"act of agreeing"
disagree	**dis**	agree		"not" or "opposite of agree"
disagree**ment**	**dis**	agree	**ment**	"opposite of agreement"

Read the words in the chart. Decide if a prefix, suffix, or both have been added to the base word. Then write the word parts in the correct columns.

Word	Prefix	Base Word	Suffix
1. disobey			
2. careful			
3. proudly			
4. acceptable			
5. refillable			
6. premeasure			
7. distrustful			
8. settlement			

Read the words in the box. Sort them under the correct base word below.

helper	protection	respected	unprotected	respectable
helpless	unhelpful	protector	disrepectful	

9. help

_____

_____

_____

10. protect

_____

_____

_____

11. respect

_____

_____

_____

Prefixes

A **prefix** is a word part that is added to the beginning of a base word. Adding a prefix creates a new word by adding to the meaning of the base word. Recognizing a prefix can help you read and understand an unknown word.

This chart lists some prefixes and their meanings.

Prefix	Meaning	Example
in-	"not"	**in**visible
co-	"with" or "together"	**co**pilot
mis-	"wrongly"	**mis**lead
en-	"cause to be" or "to make"	**en**rich

Join each prefix and base word. Write the new word on the first line. Then write the meaning of the new word on the second line.

1. mis + understanding _____

_____

2. in + correct _____

_____

3. co + exist _____

_____

4. en + able _____

_____

5. in + capable _____

_____

Use three of the new words from the list above in sentences of your own.

6. _____

7. _____

8. _____

Suffixes

A **suffix** is a word part or syllable that is added to the end of a base word. A suffix creates a new word by adding to the meaning of a base word. Recognizing a suffix can help you read and understand an unknown word.

This chart lists some suffixes and their meanings.

Suffix	Meaning	Example
-less	"without"	use**less**
-like	"resembling"	life**like**
-y	"full of" or "having"	mess**y**
-ity	"state or condition of"	real**ity**
-ive	"able to" or "tending"	creat**ive**

Join each base word and suffix. Write the new word on the first line. Then write the meaning of the new word beneath it.

1. hope + less _____

_____

2. health + y _____

_____

3. humid + ity _____

_____

4. dream + like _____

_____

5. adapt + ive _____

_____

Use one of the new words from the list above in a sentence of your own.

6. _____

_____

268   Foundational Skills Handbook

Latin and Greek Roots

Many English words have Latin or Greek roots. A **root** is a word part that has meaning, but it is not always a word on its own. Knowing the meaning of a word's Latin or Greek root can help you read and understand it.

*A smart shopper will **inspect** a product carefully before buying.*

The word *inspect* has the Latin root *spect*, which means "see" or "look."

Study these Latin and Greek roots and their meanings.

Root	Meaning	Example
audi	"hear or listen"	audit
dict	"say or tell"	dictator
tract	"pull or draw away"	extract
astro	"star"	astronomer

Read the words in the word bank. Decide which Latin or Greek root is in each word, and then sort each word into the correct column.

attract	distract	audible	predict
astronaut	auditorium	dictate	astronomy

audi	dict	tract	astro
_____	_____	_____	_____
_____	_____	_____	_____

Choose the word from the box above that best completes each sentence. Think about the meaning of the root to make sure the word makes sense.

1. The cookie crumbs will _____ ants and flies.

2. It was her dream to become a(n) _____ and travel in space.

3. Graduation was held in the _____ because of the weather.

4. A meteorologist uses many tools to _____ the weather.

Open and Closed Syllables

A **syllable** is a word part that has one vowel sound. Breaking longer words into syllables can make them easier to read. Here are some rules to help you.

When there is only one consonant between two vowels in a word, divide the word before the consonant and try the long vowel sound. This is called an **open syllable**.

Example: music → mu-sic

Sometimes dividing a word this way doesn't work; instead, you must divide the word after the consonant and try the short vowel sound. This is called a closed syllable.

Example: signal → sig-nal

If you divide the word *signal* before the consonant (si-gnal) and try the long vowel sound, you will not pronounce the word correctly. However, if you divide it after the consonant (sig-nal) and try the short vowel sound, you will pronounce the word correctly.

Write each word, dividing it into syllables with a hyphen. The first one has been done for you.

1. jungle _____jun-gle_____
2. human _____
3. clover _____
4. shiver _____
5. punish _____
6. declare _____

Read each sentence. Then divide the underlined words into syllables on the lines below the sentence.

7. The napkins and a platter of vegetables are on the table.

_____

8. Focus your attention on the basic problem.

_____

9. The vibrant colors of the textile caught my attention.

_____

Syllables with Vowel Teams

Breaking longer words into syllables can help you read the words. A syllable has one vowel sound, but that vowel sound may be spelled with more than one letter. The rules below tell you when you can divide the letters that stand for the vowel sound.

- Some words have two vowels that make one sound. These **vowel teams** stay together in a syllable. These vowel teams include *ai, ea, ei, ie, oi, oy,* and *au.*

creature	sweater	royal	autumn
cr**ea**-ture	sw**ea**t-er	r**oy**-al	**au**-tumn
explain	receive	believe	appoint
ex-pl**ai**n	re-c**ei**ve	be-l**ie**ve	ap-p**oi**nt

- Some words have two vowels together that make separate sounds. For these words, divide the word into syllables between the two vowels.

diet	poem	duet	create
d**i**-**e**t	p**o**-**e**m	d**u**-**e**t	cr**e**-**a**te

Write each word, dividing it into syllables with a hyphen. The first one has been done for you.

1. feature _____fea-ture_____

2. neon _____

3. faucet _____

4. beneath _____

5. dial _____

6. relief _____

7. riot _____

8. fluid _____

9. remain _____

10. giant _____

11. science _____

12. deceive _____

Syllables with *r*-Controlled Vowels

Recognizing spelling patterns in syllables can help you break down words into smaller parts. When a vowel is followed by the letter *r*, the letter *r* changes the sound of the vowel. The vowel and the *r* appear in the same syllable.

forest	dirty	bury	fever
f**or**-est	d**ir**t-y	b**ur**-y	fev-**er**

Read each word. Underline the letters that stand for the *r*-controlled vowel sound. Then divide the word into syllables on the line next to it. The first one has been done for you.

1. circle _____cir-cle_____

2. moral _____

3. spirit _____

4. cherish _____

5. plural _____

6. storage _____

7. florist _____

8. sterilize _____

9. glorify _____

10. experiment _____

Choose the word from the list above that best completes each sentence. Then take turns reading the sentences with a partner.

11. We use the attic and basement for _____.

12. I _____ the gifts from my family and friends.

13. The word *mice* is the _____ of the word *mouse*.

14. The beautiful flowers were delivered by the _____.

15. His team _____ encouraged the players to do their best.

16. We must _____ the glass jars to get rid of any bacteria.

17. The scientist conducted a(n) _____ to test her idea.

18. There is always a(n) _____ to the story in a fable.

Words with Silent Consonants

You can often figure out an unfamiliar word by sounding out the letters in the word. Sometimes words have **silent consonants**. Learning rules for reading silent consonants will help you read and understand these words.

- When the letters *ght* are together in a word, the letters *gh* are silent.

  fi**ght**   bri**ght**   ti**ght**

- When a word begins with the letters *kn*, the *k* is silent.

  knuckle   **kn**ead   **kn**ow

- When the letters *gn* are together in a syllable of a word, the letter *g* is silent.

  gnat   **gn**aw   forei**gn**

- When a word ends with the letters *mb*, the letter *b* is silent.

  la**mb**   cru**mb**   li**mb**

Read each sentence. Find the word or words that have silent consonants and underline the silent letters. The first one has been done for you.

1. I k<u>new</u> we were in trouble when I saw the danger si<u>g</u>n.

2. The night sky was so clear, it was easy to find constellations.

3. We set out early in the morning to climb Mount Baker.

4. The plumber hit his right thumb against the pipe.

5. I couldn't loosen the knot because my fingers were numb from the cold.

6. A bear might frighten the sleeping campers.

7. I hoped my teacher wouldn't assign any homework over the weekend.

8. She spent the afternoon with her grandmother, learning how to knit a scarf.

Practicing Fluency

Read the following excerpt from a retelling of a Japanese folk tale. Use the checklist at the bottom of the page to help guide your reading.

The Envious Stonecutter

from a Japanese Folk Tale

Koji, a simple stonecutter, was chipping away at a mountain one afternoon when a wealthy prince paraded by. Koji wept with envy for a grander life, so he appealed to the spirits. "Please, can you change me into a prince?" he begged. The spirits agreed to grant Koji's wish.

Koji the prince enjoyed the comforts of his beautiful home and garden. One day, though, after the sun scorched his prized blossoms, Koji felt envious again. "Kindly spirits! Since the sun outshines any prince, I beg to become the sun!" he pleaded. And so it came to be.

As the sun, Koji suddenly grew prideful. He boasted by blistering the earth until its creatures howled for relief. Only the mountaintops were not scorched by his rays.

When Koji saw the mountains unharmed, his envy returned. He begged to become a mountain. But the next morning, Koji awoke to find a stonecutter chipping away at his base. Once more his longing led him to call to the spirits, "Oh, if I were only a man!"

Now read the story aloud to a partner. Use the checklist below and your understanding of the story to guide your reading.

Reading Checklist

☐ Does my voice go up if there is a question mark? Does it get stronger if there is an exclamation point? Do I pause for periods and commas?

☐ How should a character's thoughts or words affect how I read?

☐ How does the tone or mood of the story—suspenseful, scary, sad, happy—change the way I read? (Remember, the tone or mood can change more than once in a story.)

Writing Handbook

STEP 1: Planning. 276

STEP 2: Drafting 278

STEP 3: Revising 279

STEP 4: Editing 281

STEP 5: Producing,
Publishing, and Presenting. . 283

This year, you will write a fictional narrative, an informative/explanatory essay, an opinion piece, an evidence-based essay, and a research report. This handbook is your guide to writing all these types of texts. It takes you through steps of the writing process, which help you move from ideas to a finished piece of writing. Once you know the steps, you can use them for any kind of writing.

STEP 1 Planning

Let's say you are going to write an opinion piece about whether we can learn from the actions of heroes, both real and fictional. Good writing begins with planning. To plan, begin by asking yourself some questions.

- **What** am I writing?

  You are writing an opinion piece. This type of essay takes a stand on an issue and supports it with strong reasons. It is nonfiction because it does not tell a story, but instead argues for a position.

- **Why** am I writing? What is my **purpose**?

  Your purpose for writing is your reason for writing. For this assignment, your purpose is to persuade, or to convince others of your opinion. You will do this by providing strong reasons that explain why we can or cannot learn from the actions of heroes.

- **Who** is my audience? Who will read my writing?

  In this case, your audience is anybody who is interested in the subject of heroes as examples of good behavior.

  Now you are ready to think of ideas and organize them. An outline is one way to plan.

- Begin with your **topic.**

  For informational text, begin by thinking about your topic, or the central idea of your writing. In an opinion essay, your topic is your opinion on a specific issue. Ask yourself, "Can we learn from the actions of heroes—even fictional ones?" The answer to this question is your position, or point of view, on the subject.

  For a fictional narrative, begin by thinking of a problem characters might face, as well as the solution to that problem.

- Then add **details**.

  For an opinion piece, provide reasons, facts, and examples that support your point of view. Many of these may come from your own ideas and experiences, but some may require research.

  For a fictional narrative, you would add characters, setting, and plot events to the basic idea for a story.

RESEARCH TIP

For this topic, part of the information you need may come from reading you have done. You can use books, magazines, online sources, and even interviews with other people as sources of information about real-life and fictional heroes. Be sure to take notes from the sources you use. Sort the information in the notes to help you organize your writing.

Here's what an outline for your opinion essay on heroes might look like. This outline shows six paragraphs—one for the introduction, four for the subtopics in the explanation, and one for the conclusion.

Heroes Help Us

I. Introduction
   Topic: Heroes help us. They teach us how to overcome obstacles and solve problems. Even fictional heroes can help us learn ways of dealing with life's challenges.

II. Supporting Reasons
   Subtopic 1: Brave people
   Facts: _____
   _____

Subtopic 2: Leaders
Facts: _____
_____

Subtopic 3: Inventors
Facts: _____
_____

Subtopic 4: Fictional heroes
Facts: _____
_____

III. Conclusion _____

PLANNING TOGETHER

You may want to plan your writing with a partner. Having a question-and-answer session with a partner can help you to clarify your ideas. You might brainstorm together. Let one idea lead to the next.

STEP 2 Drafting

When you draft, you do the actual writing of your essay. Many writers use a computer to write drafts. Follow your outline, but don't worry about making everything perfect. Just write and get your ideas down!

Here is a handwritten draft of an opinion piece about how heroes help us. This is a great start!

Heroes Help Us

Heroes help us. They teach us how to overcome obstacles and how to solve problems. Even fictional heroes can do this.

Real people who show bravery teach us. For example, think of that brave patriot Paul Revere. He faced the dangers of capture or death but he didn't fail to act. He believed in the cause of freedom so strongly. He rode all night to warn others of a threat to freedom.

Leaders teach us many lessons to. Look at how Martha Washington helped soldiers during the Revolutionary War. Her assistance meant they could keep fighting for independence.

Inventors provide us with excellent examples of how to work toward a goal. Many of them experience failure many times before they succeed. They keep at it, though. They do not give up until they achieve their goal.

Even fictional heroes. Writers tell stories about people facing problems. We can learn from how they work with others. We can see how they handle those problems.

Reading about heroes, both real and fictional, helps us see how some people met challenges. Heroes give us important lessons in how to live.

STEP 3 Revising

During this step, you think about how to make your writing better. This step is about ideas, not about details like spelling and grammar. Use the items in the checklist below to focus your ideas. Then make changes on your computer or on a handwritten copy. If you are using pencil and paper, make a fresh copy.

REVISING TOGETHER

- You can work with a partner to revise your work. Have your partner read your draft and use the checklist below to give you feedback. Use your partner's feedback to revise your draft.

- Finally, read your revised draft aloud to yourself or to your partner. See if you want to make any more improvements.

REVISING CHECKLIST

Ideas and Voice

- ☐ Do all of my reasons support my opinion?
- ☐ Have I developed my ideas by including enough facts and examples?
- ☐ Have I used information and evidence from my research?
- ☐ Does my writer's voice sound interesting and persuasive?

Organization and Coherence

- ☐ Does my introduction state my topic clearly?
- ☐ Have I grouped related ideas to support my purpose?
- ☐ Have I used linking words such as *in addition* and *for example* to connect my reasons to my opinion?
- ☐ Are all of my sentences in a logical order?
- ☐ Do I have a strong concluding section that relates to my opinion?
- ☐ Have I used a variety of sentence types?

Word Choice

- ☐ Have I used precise words?
- ☐ Have I avoided using the same words over and over?
- ☐ Do my words bring my ideas to life?

Here is a draft with notes for revisions. To see the revised draft, turn to page 282.

I want to make my second sentence more specific.

Heroes ~~Help~~ Us
Teach

Heroes help us. They teach us *many lessons like* how to overcome obstacles and how to solve problems. Even fictional heroes can do this.

Real people who show bravery teach us. For example, think of that brave patriot Paul Revere. He faced the dangers of capture or death but he didn't fail to act. ~~He~~ believed in the cause of freedom so strongly. ~~He~~ rode all night
Because he *he*
to warn others of a threat to freedom.

Leaders teach us many lessons to. Look at how Martha Washington helped soldiers during the Revolutionary War. Her work meant a lot to them.

I want to use a more precise word than "work" that connects to the idea of helping and explains more clearly how her help mattered.

Inventors provide us with excellent examples of how to work toward a goal. Many of them experience failure many times before they succeed. They ~~keep~~ at it, though they do not give up until
trying
they achieve their goals.

Even fictional heroes. Writers tell stories about people which face problems. (We can learn from how they work with others.) We can see how they handle those problems. Reading about heroes, both real and fictional, ~~helps~~ us see how some people met
can help
challenges. *In this way, heroes* ~~Heroes~~ give us important lessons in how to live.

I need to move this sentence to make the order more logical.

STEP 4 Editing

This step is about making your writing correct. Now is the time to focus on grammar, punctuation, and spelling. Read your revised draft carefully. Sometimes it helps to read it aloud. Use the Editing Checklist below and the Proofreading Marks chart on page 282 to correct errors in your writing on the computer or in your handwritten draft.

Always proofread and correct your own work. Seeing your own mistakes can be difficult, though, so asking a partner to help check your work can help.

EDITING CHECKLIST

Sentences
☐ I have corrected any sentence fragments or run-on sentences.
☐ I have not left out any words, and I have deleted any extra words.
☐ I have used a variety of sentence types.

Grammar
☐ The subject and verb of every sentence agree.
☐ The verb tense stays the same throughout.
☐ I have placed any adjectives in the correct order.
☐ Pronouns match the nouns they replace.
☐ I have used coordinating and subordinating conjunctions correctly.
☐ I have formed and used prepositional phrases correctly.

Mechanics
☐ Every sentence begins with a capital letter and ends with the correct punctuation mark.
☐ Commas, quotation marks, and other punctuation marks are used correctly, and no marks are missing.
☐ The title and all proper nouns are capitalized.
☐ Paragraphs are indented.

Spelling
☐ I have used a dictionary to check spellings I am unsure about.
☐ I have correctly used frequently confused words, such as homophones (words that sound the same, like *their/there/they're*).

WRITING HANDBOOK

Heroes Teach Us

Heroes teach us many lessons, such as how to overcome obstacles and how to solve problems. We can even learn ~~simalar~~ lessons from fictional heroes.

For example, think of that brave ~~P~~atriot Paul Revere. He faced the dangers of capture or death but he ~~didn't~~ (did not) fail to act. Because he believed in the cause of freedom so strongly, he rode all night to warn others of a threat to freedom.

Leaders teach us many lessons ∧(too) ~~to.~~ Look at how Martha Washington helped soldiers during the Revolutionary War. Her assistance meant they could keep fighting for independence.

Inventors also provide us with excellent examples of how to work toward a goal. Many of them experience failure many times before they succeed. They keep trying, though⊙≡they do not give up until they achieve their goals.

Even fictional heroes∧ (can teach us valuable lessons). Writers tell stories about people ~~which~~ who face problems. We can see how they handle those problems. We can learn from how they work with others.

Reading about heroes, both real and fictional, can help us see how some people met challenges. In this way, heroes teach us important lessons about how to live.

STEP 5 Producing, Publishing, and Presenting

Now that you've worked so hard on your writing, it's time to share it with others! Think about how your writing looks. Is it neatly handwritten, or typed and printed from a computer?

Would images add interest or important information?

- photographs
- illustrations

Would other text features make your ideas easier to understand?

- headings and subheadings • diagrams • graphs • charts • maps

Think about the final form of your writing. Be sure the way you present the final version of your work fits your purpose and audience.

Once you finish a piece of writing, you might be asked to share it with classmates in a speech or other presentation. When you shift from written English to spoken English, you may make some changes to give your speech more of a natural flow. Follow these rules to make your oral presentation effective.

> **DIGITAL CONNECTION**
>
> Technology makes it easy to present your writing to a bigger audience, especially on the Internet.

- Determine how formal or informal you need to be. Use language that fits your audience and the occasion.
- Use visuals as needed to support what you say.
- Speak clearly and loudly enough for everyone to hear.
- Speak slowly enough so that everyone can understand you.
- Change the pitch, rate, and loudness of your voice to express your ideas, show emphasis, and create an emotional effect.
- Make your gestures and facial expressions match your words.
- Ask your audience if they have any questions. Listen carefully and answer politely. Take time to think before you respond.

> **LISTENING TIPS**
>
> - Keep your eyes on the presenter, and focus your mind on the ideas.
> - Make connections from what you hear to what you already know.
> - Take notes. Include questions you want to ask.
> - Try to picture the things that are described.

GLOSSARY

A

anticipation excited waiting

assemble gather together

audibly able to be heard

B

bargain deal; getting something cheaply

basin valley; hollowed-out area of land

bedrock a solid layer of rock deep underground

biography the story of someone's life

brawn size and strength

C

calculate figure out using math or logic

camouflage something to let someone blend into his surroundings; disguise

cautious careful; watching out for danger

challenge try to fight

chamber closed-in space; compartment

charity understanding feelings; forgiveness

chided scolded

circumstance situation; fact

collapse falling down in exhaustion

colonist person who moves to a new area

compatible working well with

concede admit; accept

conclusion idea; decision

confederacy a group that works together

consequence result; effect

conservation saving; using less of something

continental drift movement of the continents

converted changed

coordinate location described in mathematical terms

custom habit

D

data facts; information

declined turned down

defiance disobedience; refusal to give in

democracy government by the people

demonstrates shows

derived got

destination the place where one is going

deteriorates becomes not as good

devastating horribly destructive

devoted loyal and loving toward

displacement pushed out of place; movement

disruption interruption; trouble

distort twist; make out of shape

distribution delivery; giving out

diverse having many differences

drill practice exercise

E

earthquakes shaking of the Earth's surface

electromagnetic spectrum the different sizes of waves light comes in

elude escape; keep from being caught by

emit send out

energy power; force

equipped prepared with correct tools

erosion the breaking down of rocks or land

escape velocity the speed needed to get out of Earth's gravity

exhausted very tired

explosive likely to explode or burst out

F

fault line where two pieces of the Earth's crust come together

fiery showing strong emotions and energy

fixture place to plug in a light bulb

flash flood a sudden, dangerous flood

focus clear view

foolhardy foolish

foolish silly; unwise

formation form or shape

fortifications defenses

fossil fuel power-making material created from the remains of ancient creatures

frostbite freezing of the skin

G

gale strong wind

generated created

glacier huge mass of ice

glare bright light

griddle frying pan

H

hardship difficulty; problem

hull the body of a ship

I

immensely hugely; greatly

immobile not moving

impression picture that stays in someone's mind

injustice unfairness

innovative full of new ideas; creative

inspection examination; check

intensely powerfully; strongly

interact work with or act on

L

labored worked

lacrosse a ball game invented by Native Americans

landmass large section of land

landscape countryside

language set of words a group uses to speak

lecture scold

limb arm or leg

longhouse home of great length that could house many people

M

manipulate change; handle

mantle a layer of the earth under the surface

merchant ship a ship carrying goods to be sold

miser a person who saves money and never spends it

misery unhappiness; suffering

monitor watch

morale mood

motivate encourage to act

mountain range line of mountains

N

natural disaster terrible event caused by nature

neutralize take away something's power

nonrenewable resource natural supply that can be used up

O

ominous threatening; dangerous

opportunity chance to do something

oppressed treated badly

orbital velocity the speed needed for an object to circle around a star or planet

orbiting circling around a planet or star

P

particle tiny piece

permanent lasting forever

perplexed confused

plate tectonics science that studies how continents move

prediction idea about what will happen next

principle main idea or belief

projector something that shines out light or images

promoted given a higher position or job

prospect possibility; idea

provisions food supplies

R

range difference

rash without thinking things through

refracted bent

renewable resource natural supply that will not run out or be used up

reservoir a lake used to store water

retrieve bring back

retro-reflection the action of a form of mirror that throws back light from its surface

revolution war fought to change governments

rousing energetic and inspiring

route path

S

sachem Native American leader

sandbank a ridge of sand sticking out of an ocean or a river

sandhog worker who builds water tunnels

satellite an object that circles around a planet or star

sediment dirt; soil

site place; spot

sleigh a carriage that slides over the snow

snubbed ignored; passed over

sonorous deep and booming

species type of animals

sprained hurt a joint by twisting

strife war; fighting; trouble

supply shaft tunnel or tube that carries materials from one place to another

sustainable able to keep going; lasting

symbolic something true in an idea rather than in fact

T

tauntingly mockingly

technology use of machines and/or computers

terrain land

thermal warm

transformed changed

treacherous dangerous

tsunami giant wave

tyrant cruel ruler

U

universe everything that exists in space

V

valve control that limits how much water flows through a pipe

venturing going

vexation annoyance; to be upset

volume loudness

W

weathering the breaking down of rocks by rain, snow, hail, and wind

A

Adages, 212
Affixes, 80
Analyzing reasons and evidence, 238–243, 250–254
Antonyms, 151, 174

B

Base words, 266

C

Capitalization, 224
Commas, 49, 134, 223
Comparing and contrasting events and topics, 162–167, 168–172
Comparing and contrasting points of view, 112–117, 118–122
Comparing and contrasting themes and topics, 200–205, 206–210
Compound sentences, 223
Connect Across Texts, 35, 79, 123, 173, 211, 255
Craft and structure, 100–105, 106–111, 112–117, 118–122, 150–155, 156–161, 162–167, 168–172

D

Describing characters, settings, and events, 24–29, 30–34
Describing text structures, 156–161, 168–172
Determining the main idea, 62–67, 74–78
Determining theme, 18–23, 30–34
Determining word meanings, 100–105, 118–122, 150–155, 168–172
Dialogue, 49, 107

Drama, 106, 107
Drawing inferences, 12–17, 30–34, 56–61, 74–78

E

Editing, 281–282
Explaining events and ideas, 68–73, 74–78
Explaining structural elements, 106–111, 118–122

F

Figurative language, 124
Formal and informal English, 184
Foundational Skills Handbook
  base words, 266
  fluency, 274
  Latin and Greek roots, 269
  phonics and word recognition, 266–273
  prefixes, 267
  r-controlled vowels, 272
  suffixes, 268
  syllables, 270–272
  words with silent consonants, 273
Fragments, 47
Frequently confused words, 185

H

Home Connect, 10, 40, 54, 84, 98, 128, 148, 178, 192, 216, 230

I

Idioms, 212
Integrating information from texts, 248–249, 250–254
Integration of knowledge and ideas, 194–199, 200–205, 206–210, 232–237, 238–243, 244–249, 250–254
Interpreting visual information, 232–237, 250–254

K

Key ideas and details, 12–17, 18–23, 24–29, 30–34, 56–61, 62–67, 68–73, 74–78

M

Making connections between texts, 194–199, 206–210
Modal auxiliaries, 186–187

O

Order of adjectives, 93
Outlining, 45, 89, 133, 183, 221, 222

P

Precise words and phrases, 92
Prefixes, 80, 267
Prepositional phrases, 90
Progressive forms of verbs, 91
Proverbs, 212
Punctuation, 137

Q

Quotation marks, 49, 134

R

r-controlled vowels, 272
Relative adverbs, 136
Relative pronouns, 135
Roots, 256, 269
Run-on sentences, 48

S

Sentences, 46–48
Setting, 106
Silent consonants, 273
Speaking and listening, 50, 94, 138, 188, 226
Spelling, 225
Suffixes, 80, 268
Summarizing, 18–23, 30–34, 62–67, 74–78
Syllables, 270–272
Synonyms, 150, 174

U

Using context clues, 36

W

Write evidence-based essays, 130–133
Write fictional narratives, 42–45
Write informative/explanatory texts, 86–89
Write opinion pieces, 180–183
Write research reports, 218–222
Writing Handbook
  drafting, 278
  editing, 281–282
  editing checklist, 281
  planning, 276–277
  proofreading marks, 282
  producing, publishing, and presenting, 283
  revising, 279–280